Chosen

The Journeys of
Bilbo and Frodo of the Shire

Anne Marie Gazzolo

Of Ages Past

CHOSEN: THE JOURNEYS OF BILBO AND FRODO OF THE SHIRE
First edition
Copyright © 2018 Anne Marie Gazzolo / Of Ages Past
ISBN: 978-0-578-40304-5
annemariegazzolo.com
ofagespast.com

To J. R. R. Tolkien,
Bilbo and Frodo Baggins,
and those who love them

And to the Writer of the Story,
for leading me to them

Praise for
Moments of Grace and Spiritual Warfare in The Lord of the Rings

In *Moments of Grace and Spiritual Warfare in The Lord of the Rings*, Anne Marie Gazzolo takes her understanding of the spiritual battles we daily face in real life and recognises the same struggles in the characters of Middle-earth. Her book is an indispensable source for the enthusiast hoping for a deeper grasp of religious themes running through Tolkien's work.

Benita J. Prins, author of *Aratar, Peredhil, and Halflings, Oh My!: The Ultimate Tolkien Quiz, Starscape*, and *Sea of Crystal, Sea of Glass*

Just to say here that I have just begun to read your *Moments of Grace* and I think that the word that comes to mind as I think of it is, beautiful. Grace is not just your subject matter but it is also in the way that you write.

Stephen C. Winter, *Wisdom from The Lord of the Rings blog*

Moments of Grace and Spiritual Warfare in The Lord of the Rings by Anne Marie Gazzolo is a wonderful book. I have read almost every book out there that explores the Christianity and spirituality of Tolkien's work and this is both one of the best in my opinion and also one of my favorites. What makes it so appealing are both its depth and its style. Ms. Gazzolo writes in a very knowledgeable way that shows her depth of understanding but also in warm way constantly reminding the reader of the life applicability of Christianity as demonstrated through Tolkien's story and characters. She does a wonderful job of showing the Christianity of Tolkien's work in all aspects and how it applies to us in our own faith journey. I highly recommend this to any reader striving daily to live their Christian faith and who has a passion for Tolkien's works.

Michael Haldas, author of *Echoes of Truth: Christianity in The Lord of the Rings*

It's an incredible book exploring Christian themes found in *Lord of the Rings*. A book about my favorite book – and my religion! Seriously, does it get better? ... I came across a preview of her book on Amazon. I read it. And then read it again. This was good stuff! I asked for the book for my birthday, and sure enough, I got it! ... it was amazing!!! Five stars all the way. ... If you haven't already, I encourage you to read *Moments of Grace and Spiritual Warfare in the Lord of the Rings*. ... trust me, you will not regret it.

H.G. Warrender, author of *The King's Decree*

While the target public is obviously spiritual, the book is attractive to read for all. It reads extremely well and is a very interesting read!

Pieter Collier, *Tolkien Library*

The Lord of the Rings tale is known quite well to all. *Moments of Grace and Spiritual Warfare in The Lord of the Rings* discusses the themes of the novel and how they can be carried to the nature of spirituality and be used to inspire readers well and through their lives, telling the stories of the characters, their personal struggles, and what we can learn from them. *Moments of Grace and Spiritual Warfare in The Lord of the Rings* is a choice pick for fans of the novels seeking a spiritual perspective on the series.

Greenspan, *Midwest Book Review*

Acknowledgements

Constance G. J. Wagner helped inspire me to write this book. She is at work on her own tribute to our favorite Ring-bearer. I thought if she could do it, so could I!

Many thanks and hobbity hugs to Joe Gilronan for so graciously allowing me to use one of his many masterpieces on the cover. Enjoy his work at twitter.com/joegilronanart!

Hobbity hugs and thanks as well to Benita J. Prins for designing the beautiful cover. If you ever have need for her services, contact her at kairosbookdesign.wixsite.com/kairosbookdesign and read her great books too!

Trudy G. Shaw has an amazing site (www.frodolivesin.us/) full of insightful essays and beautiful pictures from *The Lord of the Rings* films. Unfortunately, it is no longer updated, but it is a must-visit treasure trove for all Frodoholics, especially those interested in the spiritual aspects of the Ring-bearer's soul-journey.

Stephen C. Winter provides much food for thought about Middle-earth as a whole in his thoughtful mediations at stephencwinter.com.

Thanks also to all others who love Frodo who have taught me much about him. You will see many of them quoted throughout here.

Thanks to my family and friends for loving me through all my various obsessions. :)

Contents

Introduction

There are many journeys the souls of Hobbits, Elves, Men, and Dwarves take during the War of the Ring. None are darker or more illuminating than Frodo's trial of love. The light of this shines through, just as light and love shine through Bilbo's.

J. R. R. Tolkien mentioned in a letter to Milt Waldman *The Lord of the Rings* is seen through the eyes of hobbits "to exemplify most clearly a recurrent theme: the place in 'world politics' of the unforeseen and unforeseeable acts of will, and deeds of virtue of the apparently small, ungreat, forgotten in the places of the Wise and Great (good as well as evil)" (*Letters* 160).　　But not all the Wise and Great are ignorant of the special value hobbits have.

"Bilbo was specially selected by the authority and insight of Gandalf as *abnormal*: he had a good share of hobbit virtues: shrewd sense, generosity, patience and fortitude, and also a strong 'spark' yet unkindled. The story and its sequel are . . . about the achievements of specially graced and gifted individuals. I would say . . . 'by ordained individuals, inspired and guided by an Emissary to ends beyond their individual education and enlargement'" (*Letters* 365). Frodo is a "Hobbit of exceptional character. Frodo is also a friend of the Elves, knowledgeable in their language and a lover of their songs. Like Bilbo - or any other good Hobbit - Frodo loves good food and simple comforts, but he is also thoughtful and curious and has a wisdom and strength of character that set[s] him apart" (Gardner et al. 10). What also differentiates the Bagginses from many of their fellow hobbits is their long-suppressed and unhobbit-like thirst for adventure. "Bilbo himself recognizes Frodo as his heir to more than just the good life of Bag End. Rather, he senses in him a questing soul to match, perhaps even surpass, his own" (Wagner, "War" 339). Patricia Meyer Spacks mentions several other traits they share:

> Both hobbits possess the same morality, share the
> same virtues. They are unfailingly loyal, to

companions and to principles. They are cheerful in the face of adversity, persistent to the point of stubbornness in the pursuit of a goal, deeply honest, humble in their devotion to those they consider greater than they. And as their most vital attributes they possess 'naked will and courage.' (83)

This last virtue comes from the northern mythologies Tolkien admired and speaks of in his essay, "Beowulf: The Monsters and the Critics." It is no surprise then hobbits receive the most important roles in *The Lord of the Rings* and its predecessor. In the unfinished tale "The Quest of Erebor," Gandalf says he knew the type of hobbit he wanted: a combination of adventurous Took and grounded Baggins. He is well aware the choice of Bilbo was not his alone. He was himself selected as the instrument through which another let His will be known (331). The One who truly chose Bilbo did so for a far greater reason than mere burglar. In *The Fellowship of the Ring*, Gandalf makes it clear Frodo was set apart as well.

Bilbo discovers his long-buried desire for adventure prepares and strengthens him for a life-changing journey. All of Middle-earth benefits as he exercises this atrophied muscle. The Shire and Bag End lend power to Frodo to confront and overcome his fears to embrace his awe-ful calling. Richard Mathews notes the special virtue of hobbit dwellings: "This is 'comfort' in its most deeply rooted sense, as it come into Middle English from the Latin and Old French: 'to strengthen'" (8). Bilbo is strengthened *by* his adventures, and Frodo is strengthened *for* them.

Ryan Marotta notes, "At its heart, Bilbo's journey is a spiritual one, centered equally on his own development and the transfiguration of the world around him. By allowing himself to grow, Bilbo participates in the growth of Middle-earth" (76). Corey Olsen observes, "Bilbo's experiences from his journey . . . will do more than change and shape him personally, helping him to value his peaceful life more when he returns to it. His story will reach out to influence others, granting them a measure of the wisdom that Bilbo himself is gaining through his memorable, if often painful, experiences" (216). Both of these remarks easily apply to Frodo as well. Constance G. J. Wagner's words about Frodo are equally true of Bilbo:

> . . . all come away changed because of their connection with this one seemingly simple soul.
>
> . . .
>
> Frodo's freely accepted role as Ringbearer with all its attendant burdens regarding the fate of Middle-earth, makes him a *channel of grace* - first for those most intimately connected with him; then at the end of his soul journey, for all of Middle-earth. ("Sacramentum" 83; emphasis in original)

Bilbo has no idea his terrifying experience in the goblin tunnels leads to his vocation as Ring-finder. Indeed, not even Tolkien realized at first all the implications of this. Frodo is aware he is chosen and a doom placed upon him. He does not know who did this or why. Nonetheless both hobbits fearfully and courageously follow the paths laid out for them. *The Hobbit's* narrator rightly praises Bilbo as he approaches Smaug: "Going on from there was the bravest thing he ever did. The tremendous things that happened afterwards were as nothing compared to it. He fought the real battle in the tunnel alone . . ." (*Hobbit* 264).

Bilbo and Frodo repeatedly face this spiritual warfare, the war with the self over fear. As they push past imagined limits, they discover much about strengths they did not know they had. Jim Ware notes, "Oddly enough, the God-directed inner self seems to *require* conflict for the development of a keen spiritual edge" (138; emphasis in original). Bilbo and Frodo demonstrate this as each trial overcome fortifies them for the next. "Bilbo was blessed, but that doesn't mean his path was easy. . . . Bilbo was called upon to endure great hardships, sometimes almost more than he could bear. He ended up in tight situations again and again, and he repeatedly faced danger. But because he *was* blessed, he was eventually delivered from all his troubles" (Strauss 182-183; emphasis in original). These words describe Frodo as well.

Ilúvatar does not entrust the destruction of the Ring to the strong and mighty. No, He chooses from among the 'weak.' The destinies of both Bilbo and Frodo are "meant" to be intertwined with the Ring's fate. But both Baggineses, not to mention Sam, must choose to cooperate or not with this doom. Bilbo could have dug in his heels and decided to stay home and not follow the dwarves. He could have gone but decided to slay Gollum or refused to give up the Ring after his birthday party.

The Quest Frodo undertakes is no ordinary fairy tale to seek to gain something of great power. His task is to lose what Bilbo found: in fact to face and to even embrace the peril of the loss of himself. During this long and torturous trial, he could have refused his calling at any number of points. Indeed, he tries to do so, but he always returns to it. Even with his knowledge of the Ring's evil, he could have chosen to claim it or surrendered to despair and abandoned the Quest. Any of these or other myriad choices the Bagginses make along the way could have destroyed their vocations and Middle-earth with it. Instead they choose to throw away the comfortable, peaceful time they enjoy in the Shire, Rivendell, and other havens to go further into danger. Frodo does not will to do this because the consequences of refusal are too horrific to imagine, but because he *can* imagine them.

In Frodo's devotion to the mission entrusted to him, he gives a wonderful example of total abandonment to Providence. He does not believe he has the strength for the arduous task ahead of him, but he goes forward in trustful obedience. Trudy G. Shaw notes his actions demonstrate "not only . . . courage but also radical faith in that Caller whose existence he knows only from the fact that he's been called" ("Paradox").

Dwight Longenecker notes, "Tolkien presents us with a Christian hero and type of a Christian saint because Frodo, in his faithful obedience and humility, lives out the way of sacrificial love" ("Frodo").

[Frodo] does not feel the thrill of adventure and does not yearn for glory and recognition. Rather, he views the quest as merely a burden, and a seemingly impossible one at that.

He maintains a bearing of great humility throughout the novel, and we sense that it is this very humility, along with his strength of character, that may enable him to succeed in the end. (Gardener et al. 89)

How lovely Frodo's melody in the Great Music sounds, as more and more he offers himself up in obedience. The refining fire of the Quest burns away who he was and transforms him slowly and agonizingly from "a simple hobbit into an epic hero bound upon a wheel of fire" (Moorman 212). He chooses for evil to consume him rather than the world and receives particular grace to endure this torment. "Where evil conquers, there is filth, devastation and death. Frodo's great sacrifice is to have taken the weight of that foulness upon him in order to cleanse the land for the return of life" (Gunton 134). Anna Smol observes:

> In order to show adequately the physical deterioration that Frodo's body undergoes, Tolkien establishes a contrasting beginning point so that we can judge how the healthy, red-cheeked hobbit can become the blind, twitching, slumped and starved body, unable to move on his own, on Mount Doom. The hobbit who laughs with pleasure at the smell of mushrooms rising from Mrs. Maggot's basket or the lively fellow who saves the best wine for himself and his closest friends, downing the last glass of Old Winyards with gusto as he says good-bye to Bag End becomes, when he reaches his goal, the being who cannot smell, taste, hear, or see anything except the Wheel of Fire. (40-41)

Ginna Wilkerson likens Frodo's agony as akin to one who suffers from domestic violence (83-91). But unlike a battered person who may escape, he knows he cannot leave his abuser. He must keep his assailant with him in the hope to destroy it before it destroys him. He defeats his adversary the only way he can. He chooses to take one more breath, one more step toward the one place only he and the One who chose him can bring the Ring to.

And this while he believes it will also bring him to his own destruction.

Through increasingly horrific suffering and devouring despair, the Ring-bearer drains his cup of sorrows to the dregs. He does not let go of his cross until the end when he is overcome and cannot carry it any further. He is a hollow shell, stripped even of his memories. A terribly discordant note threatens to overwhelm Frodo's part in the symphony that already absorbed the other miscues which tried to impose themselves. Then it, too, is absorbed. Three small, starved, mortal beings, Frodo, Sam, and Gollum, bring down a mighty, immortal creature. In their weakness and seeming insignificance, they accomplish what no army could have. Words of Charles Stanley apply to Frodo, Sam, Gandalf, and Aragorn: "Supernatural ministry calls for a total giving of one's love, time, compassion, gifts, and loyalty. It means being in a position where nothing is held back" (82). Well does Gandalf name the Ring-bearer and Sam, "*Bronwe athan Harthad* and *Harthad Uluithiad,* Endurance beyond Hope and Hope unquenchable" (*Sauron Defeated* 62). Barry Gordon notes:

> Middle-earth is saved through the priestly self-sacrifice of the hobbit, Frodo; through the wisdom and guidance of Gandalf the wizard; and through the mastery of Aragorn, the heir of kings. . . . as each of these agents progressively responds to the demands of the primary office to which he has been called, so he grows in power and grace, and begins to exercise the other two redemptive offices in greater depth.
>
> . . .
>
> Always, in this trial, Frodo remains the Lamb whose only real strength is his capacity to make an offering of himself. ("Kingship")

Patrick Grant notes, "As the tale ends, Frodo has achieved a heroic sanctity verging on the otherwordly" (174). Verlyn Flieger observes,"For [Frodo] is that most moving of hero types, one whose sacrifice benefits everyone but himself, one who, in saving the world (as Frodo does through Sam and Gollum) loses it" ("Missing" 230).

As Gandalf says of Bilbo, "There is a lot more in him than you guess, and a deal more than he has any idea of himself" (*Hobbit* 21). Decades later, the wizard notes the same applies to Frodo. They, as well as the invaluable and irreplaceable Sam, Merry, and Pippin, prove again and again what marvelous beings hobbits are.

An Unlikely Hero

Gandalf recounts in "Erebor" how the twin threats of Sauron and Smaug greatly troubled him. He chances upon Thorin Oakenshield on the way to the Shire. Wizard and dwarf acknowledge they felt a call to seek out the other. At Thorin's home, they discuss the problem of the dragon, and then Gandalf leaves again for the Shire.

Bilbo Baggins impressed the wizard during a previous visit. The hobbit had not yet reached maturity and was full of curiosity about the outside world. Gandalf thinks he would be the ideal person to accompany the dwarves on their trip to Smaug's mountain. In *The Hobbit*, the wizard meets the adult Bilbo and learns the painfully incompatible lineage of completely predictable Baggins and scandalously adventurous Took has the former firmly in charge. ". . . Bilbo has become entrenched in his routine, as if he has allowed himself to become so comfortable with the 'expected' that he has lost any sense of individual will" (Marotta 73). Devin Brown notes "an inordinate need for predictability, safety, and comfort" defines and confines the hobbit (83).

Within this straitjacket, however, Bilbo's adventurous dreams still exist. All they need is the proper match to flare up. The unexpected and unwanted arrival of Gandalf and dwarves provides this. On some level, the wizard notes in "Erebor," the hobbit himself is aware adventure may come to call at some point in his life, whether he wants it or not: ". . . I guessed that he wanted to remain 'unattached' for some reason deep down which he did not understand himself - or would not acknowledge, for it alarmed him. He wanted, all the same, to be free to go when the chance came, or he had made up his courage" (331).

Bilbo's slumbering Tookishness stirs after Gandalf arrives at Bag-End. It thrills to remember the legends surrounding the wizard. Anne Petty remarks, "Gandalf makes it fairly clear that he is answering some inner call from Bilbo himself and that his appearance with Thorin and company is only giving Bilbo what he has silently asked for" (266). His Baggins side, however, flatly refuses the call to adventure.

The hobbit dismisses the wizard and thinks he managed to dodge the bullet. He learns, much to his dismay, he has not. As he plays host to thirteen dwarves who walk and tumble into his home, the Baggins part of him tries to deny the sneaking suspicion an adventure has indeed burst upon him. The song of the dwarves kindles anew the cold ashes of the Tookish longing for excitement.

> It is at this moment that his spirit is awakened by his imagination, freeing his will from the enslavement of routine and igniting a desire within him to seek an existence outside of the expected. His body may not leave Bag-End until the next morning, but it is here that his heart embarks, leaving the comfort and confines of the Shire for the unknown world beyond. Through the fundamental change that takes place in Bilbo's soul, his departure becomes an act of free will, rather than simply the result of an involuntary 'nudge out of the door.' This distinction is essential to the hobbit's journey, as it is Bilbo's willpower that will come to define him. (Marotta 74)

Stephen C. Winter notes, "Both Bilbo and Gandalf are called by a longing for beauty to risk all to preserve it in the world. For Gandalf this longing has been a conscious discipline sustained throughout his long pilgrimage in Middle-earth; for Bilbo it is a longing that is awakened within him almost against his will. . . . Sauron could not be overcome without both Gandalf and Bilbo" ("Sustained").

The Baggins side is no less imaginative than the Tookish, but this causes it anxiety rather than excitement. It gets so overwrought by Thorin's declaration the journey to the Lonely Mountain may be fatal, it cries out in terror and collapses. This does not endear him to the dwarves. Bilbo does not seem at all the adventurous type the wizard told them to expect. After the hobbit revives to overhear this, his Tookishness rears up to defend his honor. He agrees with the conviction the dwarves came to the wrong home and admits his lack of understanding about what their quest is about. In spite of all this, and much to the dismay of his Baggins side, Bilbo commits himself to their desperate venture. Gandalf twice says he deliberately chose the hobbit for it. He assures them all Bilbo will rise to the occasion.

The wizard brings out a map of the Mountain and a key to a secret entrance. For the third time, Gandalf speaks of Bilbo as "the chosen and selected burglar" (*Hobbit* 26). Both sides of the hobbit continue to war within him. Even though the Tookish part remains in control, the practical Baggins side asks all sorts of questions. If it is to be dragged into some great danger, it does not want to run willy-nilly into it.

After the dwarves settle matters, Bilbo turns his hole into a bed and breakfast. The exhausted hobbit falls asleep to the sound of Thorin's voice raised in song. This does not prove conducive to good dreams.

Bilbo wakes late the next morning and finds himself alone. His Baggins side is glad, but his Tookishness feels let down. He returns to his peaceful, safe, and stale life. But not for long. Gandalf and adventure barge back in upon him. The wizard directs the hobbit's attention to the note Thorin left expecting him to join the dwarves. Before Bilbo can pack, and more importantly, before his Baggins side can stop him, he rushes out to meet his companions almost before he knows he left.

Thus begins Bilbo's long descent from respectability as a solid, predictable, and unadventurous hobbit. It also starts his long ascent to gain the respect of the dwarves. He enjoys his journey at first. But then they leave the Shire behind and enter the Lone-lands. As the land and weather change for the worst, he longs for home. Bilbo is a figure alone. He does not fit in outside his homeland, and he does not fit in with the dwarves.

Yet for all the hobbit's wishful thinking and misery, his Baggins side does not have the strength to smother his Tookishness. The dwarves volunteer him to investigate a distant light in a dark forest. The same hobbit who collapsed in terror at the mere thought of danger now moves forward toward unknown perils. Rather than prudently return before three grumpy trolls gathered around their campfire see him, Bilbo attempts to live up to his assigned job title.

Unfortunately, the purse he seeks to purloin alerts the creatures to his presence.

The hobbit tries to flee after an argument breaks out. But Bert so physically traumatized him, he does not get far. The trolls stop their brawl the moment Balin appears. They capture him and the other dwarves. Thorin comes last and puts up a fight. Bilbo makes a valiant but futile attempt to assist him.

Rescue comes from a mysterious voice that confuses and angers the trolls. They argue overlong as to how to cook their prisoners. After the sun comes up and turns the creatures to stone, Bilbo and Gandalf free the dwarves.

The wizard tells his companions to look around for the trolls' cave. Bilbo finds a key William lost during the fight. This is the first moment of grace (or luck as the hobbit understands it) in a remarkable string of them. Inside the cave, the Company finds the swords Orcrist and Glamdring. Bilbo gains the knife he later christens Sting. "The group only dared to venture after the light in the unknown night . . . because of their disastrous loss of supplies. Because of this, in the end, they come out richer, better equipped, and better armed. Divine providence lies underneath the entire chapter" (Timothy, "Mutton"). Before the group leaves, they help themselves to food and ale and bury gold from the trolls' hoard.

Bilbo, Gandalf, and the dwarves travel for days until they come near to the foot of the Misty Mountains. The hobbit again longs for home.

The Company continues until they reach the house of Elrond. Elves are much more to Bilbo's liking than they are to the dwarves. Corey Olsen notes, "Bilbo is not very familiar with the elves, but he both loves and fears them, a mixture of conflicting reactions that speaks to their strangeness, but also hints at something higher or greater, which Bilbo himself only imperfectly understands" (59).

Rivendell is such a wonderful place it temporarily extinguishes the hobbit's longing for home. It satisfies both his Tookish and Baggins sides. He gets all the joy of songs and tales of adventuring without bodily experiencing any of their attendant perils. He could easily spend a happy eternity here. Even the spirits of the dwarves rise.

The providential timing of this visit becomes apparent after Elrond looks at the map of Smaug's mountain on the one night the otherwise invisible runes can be seen. These give critical clues to enter the dragon's lair at a quite particular time of day and year. "...we can begin to suspect that Bilbo's adventure is being orchestrated by some power beyond the wizardry of Gandalf the Grey or the wisdom of Elrond of Rivendell" (Olsen 67).

The next day Bilbo, Gandalf, and the dwarves leave the Last Homely House. The mountains they travel through are the same ones Frodo and his companions encounter decades later. Even though Thorin's company is far north of Moria, the two journeys have similarities. Both encounter a fierce storm on the trail. Both get trapped inside the realm of their enemies and have to find their way out at great risk to their lives.

Fili and Kili find a cave for the Company to shelter in. None of them realize it is the entrance to a goblin stronghold. Luckily, they have Bilbo with them. Once they settle down for the night, a restlessness afflicts the hobbit that does not disturb the others. When he does sleep, he has nightmares. Providentially, he wakes in time to find them reality and raises the alarm. This rouses Gandalf in time to kill several goblins. Others capture Bilbo and the dwarves. At their cruel treatment, the hobbit again longs for home. This seems the worst luck, but it starts him on a vital journey. It reveals the reason Ilúvatar wanted him on the adventure, a reason veiled even from Gandalf.

After the death of the Great Goblin, and in the midst of a desperate flight from many enemies, Bilbo wonders yet again why in the world he ever decided to take part in this adventure. The goblins quietly pursue their prisoners and attack Dori at the rear, while he carries Bilbo. The hobbit falls and is knocked unconscious. He wakes alone in the pitch dark with no idea where he is.

The crucible of doubt and danger in which the hobbit's adventurous spirit is being formed and refined . . . [reaches] its hottest and most desperate point.

. . .

He has been steadily and increasingly immersed in the world of adventure . . . , but up until this point he has only been a kind of passenger, an observer. . . . Mr. Baggins . . . now finds himself . . . forced to find his way to the other side of the Misty Mountains through the complex tunnel network of the murderous goblins who are hunting for him, without any food or water or even a source of light. Bilbo must now become a real adventurer or die. (Olsen 84, 85)

The hobbit's separation from his companions provides another crucial moment in his ascendance as a key player in the history of Middle-earth. As he crawls along the floor, he happens upon a small ring. Many different choices Bilbo and others make enable him to arrive in time to pick up this particular thread of the Story as it winds its way through history. These decisions reach back as far back as Gandalf and Thorin meeting by 'chance' on the way to Bree. The wizard chooses to respond to the call he felt to decide upon Bilbo in particular and to convince the dwarves to take the hobbit along. Bilbo makes the choice to come with them. Gandalf decides to rescue the Company from the trolls and the Great Goblin. Dori chooses to carry Bilbo. Gollum chooses to throttle a goblin and unknowingly loses his precious ring. It lays there for Bilbo to come by and pick up. Gandalf makes clear the providential timing of this lynchpin event in his discussion with Frodo decades later.

Bilbo puts the ring in his pocket without much thought and crawls on. The hobbit longs once more for home. To have any hope to return there, he embraces his Tookishness and allows his long-denied dreams to become reality. Fear fills him, but it does not stop him.

The hobbit continues until he hits water. With no way to tell how deep or far across it is, he stops. He does not know he is under surveillance by an unsavory creature. That is, not until he hears it speak of how delicious he would be to eat. So meet two small beings who play such crucial roles in the fate of the Ring. Bonniejean Christensen observes:

> J. R. R. Tolkien's fallen hobbit, Gollum, is an interesting character in his own right, but the changes in his character that Tolkien made between the first edition of *The Hobbit* in the 1930s and second edition in the 1950s make him one of his most fascinating creations.
>
> . . .
>
> In *The Hobbit* he is one of a series of fallen creatures on a rising scale of terror. In *The Lord of the Rings* he is an example of the damned individual who loses his own soul because of devotion to evil (symbolized by the ring) but who, through grace, saves others. (9, 10)

In an earlier draft of *The Lord of the Rings*, Gandalf tells Frodo of Gollum's pitiable state before he met Bilbo:

> "Don't you realize that he had possessed the Ring for ages, and the torment was becoming unendurable? He was so wretched that he knew he was wretched, and had at last understood what caused it. . . . Half his mind wanted above all to be rid of the Ring, even if the loss killed him. But he hated parting with it as much as keeping it. He wanted to hand it on to someone else, and to make him wretched too." (*Treason* 24-25)

The wizard goes on to say Gollum would not give the Ring to the goblins. After Bilbo comes, the creature sees his chance. Gandalf hints at the other Power at work in his mention both Bilbo and Frodo were singled out as the Ring's guardians. Through this, Gollum's life remains safe. If anyone other than Bilbo found the fell object, it would have likely meant the wretched being's death (*Treason* 25).

Bilbo knows from stories not to reveal one's name to dragons. But the creature now before him has never appeared in any tales. The hobbit does not know to take the same precautions. He formally introduces himself and mentions his predicament. This later threatens Frodo. It also sends him on his way to play his own critical part to save Middle-earth from the peril ready to engulf it.

Gollum challenges Bilbo to a high-stakes riddle-game which reveals their respective worldviews. The hobbit speaks of life, light, and beautiful things. In retaliation, Gollum focuses for the most part on death, darkness, and decay. Bilbo likewise counters the wretched creature's despair with hope.

With the hobbit's life in immediate peril, he cannot think as clearly as he would otherwise. But he need not, as grace provides some of the answers without his conscious thought. One of them comes after Gollum starts to get out of his boat in his hasty lust to have dinner. This action disturbs a fish that leaps out onto Bilbo's feet.

With Gollum's next riddle, he really has the hobbit over a barrel. He gets back out of his boat in anticipation of victory. But once more, grace provides Bilbo the answer. In a desperate bid to ask for more time, all he gets out is the last word.

Gollum says his visitor must ask him a question. The hobbit cannot think of anything until he feels the ring he acquired. He wonders out loud, "What have I got in my pocket?" (*Hobbit* 97). Gollum thinks Bilbo addresses him and protests about a breach in the rules. But he opened the door himself in his request for a question. The hobbit sticks to his inadvertent obedience and accepts the creature's demand for three attempts to answer. After four incorrect guesses, Gollum finally cedes victory to his opponent.

The first edition of *The Hobbit* tells a different version of the well-known aftermath of the game. Originally, Gollum promises Bilbo an unspecified gift if the hobbit wins. After Bilbo does, he asks Gollum to hold up his end of the bargain. The wretched creature searches hard for the ring he means to give. He finally comes back empty-handed. Bilbo states he will let Gollum out of his promise on the condition the creature guides him out of the tunnels. Gollum does so until he is too afraid to go any further. The hobbit then continues on his own. John Rateliff notes:

> . . . we should . . . give [Gollum] his due: having lost the contest, he is pathetically eager to make good on his debt of honour ('I don't know how many times Gollum begged Bilbo's pardon'), offering a substitute reward ('fish caught fresh to eat') in place of the missing ring. Remember too that Gollum had not yet specified what the 'present' was; a less scrupulous monster might have been tempted, upon discovering the ring's absence, to substitute some other prize, such as the fish, for the unnamed prize - but not Gollum. We are thus faced with the amusing depiction of a monster who is considerably more honourable than our hero. For Bilbo soon realizes that he already has Gollum's treasure but goes ahead and demands a second prize (being shown the way out) in addition to the one he has quietly pocketed - a neat parallel to Gollum's earlier trick of 'working in two answers at once' on that final attempt to answer the last question. The narrator, moreover, applauds his duplicity . . . with spurious logic that sounds so much like special pleading that Tolkien eventually decided it was just that: Bilbo's own attempt, in writing this scene for his memoirs, to justify his claim to the ring. . . . (167)

After Tolkien discovered the ring Bilbo found was *the* Ring and learned of its terrible hold on its bearers, he knew Gollum would not willingly part with it. To correct what the hobbit transcribed in his diary, Tolkien published a second edition.

In this new and improved version, despite the fact "the riddle-game was sacred and of immense antiquity, and even wicked creatures were afraid to cheat," Bilbo considers it likely Gollum will (*Hobbit* 98). After the creatures loses, the hobbit demands Gollum adhere to the agreed upon terms and show him the exit. He is quite right to think the creature's insistence he must retrieve some gear is an excuse to disappear. The wicked being has every intention to do this and then attack the hobbit while invisible.

After Gollum slips off to his secret island, Bilbo hears him raise a great lament. "Utterly miserable as Gollum sounded, Bilbo could not find much pity in his heart . . ." (*Hobbit* 101). The creature asks again what the hobbit's pocket contains. Even though Bilbo sees no reason not to answer at this point, he refuses out of irritation with Gollum's dilly-dallying. The creature belatedly divines the answer is in fact the object "in whose shining symmetry is encased Gollum's dark soul" (O'Neill 61). He rushes back, now completely intent upon his meal.

Bilbo flees. "The ring felt very cold as it quietly slipped on to his groping forefinger" (*Hobbit* 102). This particular wording indicates the Ring is the agent at work here. Moments after the hobbit becomes invisible, he trips and falls with Gollum close behind. Bilbo's part in the Story could have ended here, but the creature passes him without realizing it. The hobbit stealthily follows in the hope his would-be murderer will unwittingly show him the exit.

Gollum comes as close as he dares to the goblin's back door and fulfills Bilbo's hope. But then he stays the hobbit's victory even as Bilbo reaches out to grasp it. The creature stops and block his prey from moving further. Gollum detects he is near, even though still invisible. A terrible desire to kill his adversary surges through Bilbo. Susan Ang notes:

> The prose of the first few sentences, with its jerky ragged rhythms, manages to suggest the panicked workings of animal instinct. This is not the mind in control, but the conscience-free surgings of adrenaline urging survival at any price. While the survival instinct is dominant, Gollum is an 'it', a 'thing'. However, the rhythm then eases into reflectiveness. Gollum is given a name in Bilbo's thoughts and becomes 'he', a person, whose 'otherness' and difference, even strangeness, are suddenly comprehended, the gulf between the two is momentarily erased as Bilbo knows what it is to be Gollum. There is no need to put out

his eyes; Gollum's days are already lightless. And so Bilbo refrains from killing him. This is a moment of immense compassion, both in the modern meaning of this word and in its original (Latin) sense: *compassio*, 'I suffer with.' (55)

The Ring provides unwitting aid here. Joe Kraus notes Bilbo's "invisibility gives him a glimpse into another's humanity. The power to see and not be seen . . . liberates him and allows him to show mercy in a way that . . . proves essential to Sauron's downfall" (246). Of course, Bilbo has no foreknowledge of the profound effects his mercy will have. His conscious mind is unaware Ilúvatar guides and guards him. Such permeates his soul, though, and inspires his will to freely choose to act in concert with his Creator's plans. He knows Gollum intends to murder him and even enables this possibility by his mercy. But rather than give into fear of what *might* happen or even is *likely* to happen, the hobbit knows he cannot, must not strike. Frodo later does not for the same reason and with far greater knowledge of Gollum's villainy. These choices allow the Bagginses to escape from shedding blood or taking a life. They preserve the purity of their souls and avoid the slow and painful spiritual death which would have occurred if they struck down their adversary without need. Gollum's defenselessness and ignorance of his danger also helps the Ring-finder to decide what action to take.

Thousands of years later, Jesus tells His followers to "love your enemies, do good to those who hate you" (Lk 6:27) and "Be compassionate as your Father is compassionate" (Lk 6:36). Bilbo and all those who show pity and mercy to Gollum already live out this wisdom. Upon this knife edge a most critical point in the history of the Ring and of all Middle-earth pivots. Louis Markos, Ray Marotta, and Fleming Rutledge give insights into this crucial moment:

> The pity that stays Bilbo's hand is a pure expression of *caritas* that is born out of Bilbo's ability to move out of himself (out of his fear, hatred, and disgust) and feel a sympathetic (even empathetic) connection with the loathsome and deceptive

Gollum. . . . Gollum . . . does not, in any human sense, deserve pity, love, or mercy. But then the pity that wells up within Bilbo at this decisive moment is not human but divine. In a flash of what can only be described as divine insight, Bilbo is enabled to see Gollum's misery though Gollum's eyes, to experience vicariously, and therefore understand, the horror of his dark, hopeless condition. It is that insight that allows him to love Gollum as a suffering thing in need of grace. . . . Bilbo takes pity on Gollum, not because he deserves pity but because Bilbo allows himself to be a conduit of a higher pity. (Markos 136-137)

This is Bilbo's defining moment of spiritual maturation, the point at which he ceases to be an ordinary hobbit and finally grows into a heroic adventurer. . . . While many heroes are praised for their feats of strength and violence, Bilbo's act of mercy anoints him as a true hero for the opposite reason: it is a willful demonstration of self-control, peace, and in its deepest meaning, love. Bilbo's simple act of compassion - his choice to preserve the life of another at the risk of his own - completes his metamorphosis from a creature of routine to a being of will, and would ultimately change the fate of Middle-earth. (Marotta 75)

Bilbo is enabled to see through Gollum's unattractive surface characteristics to his wretched underlying condition. It is a description of unredeemed humanity 'tied and bound by the chain of our sin' [Book of Common Prayer]. Bilbo trembled, we are told. Something is implicit here that will become explicit later in *The Lord of the Rings*. Bilbo sees Gollum as one might have been himself. That is why he trembles; this is the insight that produces 'a sudden understanding mixed with horror.' When we come to the Ring saga itself, we will hear a great deal more about the vital importance of *understanding*, and more still about pity and horror.

Bilbo's sense of horror is provoked not by Gollum's sliminess but by the hopelessness of his bondage. . . . 'There but for grace of God go I' is the thought that comes to Bilbo and causes him to spare Gollum's life, and this is the source of the new courage that propels him out of the tunnel into safety. It can't be stated too strongly: this brief passage in *The Hobbit* lays out the theological foundation for the climax of *The Lord of the Rings*. (Rutledge 27-28; emphasis in original)

Shortly before there was little pity in Bilbo's heart for Gollum's misery. The empathy that blossoms now is a moment of grace that blesses not only Gollum but in the end the whole world. C. S. Lewis's definition of charity easily applies: "Good and evil both increase at compound interest. That is why the little decisions you and I make every day are of such infinite importance. The smallest good act today is the capture of a strategic point from which, a few months later, you may be able to go on to victories you never dreamed of" (*Mere Christianity* 133). Bilbo's selfless act continues the cascade of events that will destroy the Ring. Because he gives pity, Gandalf has the opportunity to tell Frodo of it. Because the younger Baggins takes the wizard's words to heart, he embraces the chance to exercise the same restraint and begs Faramir to do so as well. Because Frodo teaches Sam the importance of it, the gardener chooses to extend it also. All of this enables Gollum to live to fulfill his calling as Ring-destroyer.

Bilbo leaps over Gollum with "a new strength and resolve that literally propel him back to the light he was desperate to regain. His moral choice becomes a leap of faith, a 'leap in the dark' and out of the dark, and he successfully rises above both of the dark ends that awaited him there, either to be killed by Gollum or to become him" (Olsen 108). J. R. Wytenbroek observes, "Bilbo sets his ego aside when he reaches out in compassion and pity to the undesirable and unlovable other, risking his own life rather than taking the life of that other. This action is truly heroic, and through it Bilbo is reborn from a lowly, unconfident, safety- and comfort-loving hobbit into a leader . . ." (6).

Bilbo does not know how close he is to death at Gollum's hand. He barely clears the ceiling and would have died if he fell. His enemy tries to grab him, but the Ring-finder escapes down the tunnel. Gollum fears capture by the goblins so does not pursue Bilbo. He has no idea the hobbit saved his life. Rather than gratitude, Bilbo earns undying hatred.

The darkness that devoured Gollum long before does not eclipse Bilbo's soul. But the hobbit is not safe yet. He must still get past the goblins who guard the entrance. The Ring attempts to betray him by exposing him to his enemies. "A pang of fear and loss, like an echo of Gollum's misery, smote Bilbo . . . " (*Hobbit* 108). The Ring returns to his finger. Once more, the words used in the tale are precise the fell object decides to do this, not its bearer. It saves the hobbit from capture.

In the uproar that follows, Bilbo makes a run for the door, which is now almost completely closed. The goblins find him after he gets stuck in it. In terrible fear for his life, the Ring-finder struggles until he finally gets clear. All he loses is his coat buttons. "These brass buttons are a symbol of his Baggins side. . . . They have now been stripped away, and the Tookish side has finally come out. The old Bilbo, though not completely gone, has been squeezed out amidst turmoil and adventure, and a new buttonless Bilbo emerges from here on" (Timothy, "Riddles"). Ilúvatar could have ensured the opening was big enough for the hobbit to get through without a problem. Instead Bilbo has to work hard at it. The will and courage to do this makes the exit possible and strengthens him for the trials to come.

Unexpected Friends

Bilbo marvels to see how far he traveled through the mountains. He has no inkling where his companions are. As he travels away from the goblin stronghold, the thought he should return to look for the dwarves grows on him. He can disappear now and search for them with little danger to himself. Even so, he dreads to return to the tunnels. As Sam later realizes, the Ring does not confer courage. Any such virtue must come from a heart filled with love. Bilbo knows to seek his friends is the right thing to do.

The hobbit receives his reward by simply making this difficult choice without the need to follow through. He hears voices and sees Balin look right at him with no idea he is there. Bilbo's brave and generous heart contrasts sharply with the fearful dwarves. Gandalf says they must search for the hobbit. The dwarves are more than willing to let him remain lost. His sudden reappearance astounds them all. It serves as the catalyst for the dwarves to look upon him with new respect and as an equal.

Bilbo's actions after this glad reunion show the Ring has already made some inroads into his heart and soul. He regales his companions with his adventures, but he keeps secret his new possession. This is all the Ring accomplishes for now. Gandalf points out to Frodo much later Bilbo's pity and the fact the fell object was meant to come to him are two reasons its malice did not form a deeper connection with him immediately. James Stuart Bell notes:

> . . . outside forces were at work in Bilbo's life - forces all the way up to the Creator, Ilúvatar himself. Bilbo has a destiny and a purpose, and finding the Ruling Ring is a major component. As such, he is protected from the ring's dark influences because he is already in service to a greater Will, a more powerful Master.
>
> As the apostle John says: 'The one who is in you is greater than the one who is in the world' (1 John 4:4). (101)

The Company walks for hours until they come to a clearing with an evil feel to it. The howls of wolves confirm they managed to escape one enemy only to fall prey to another. With no time to spare, the group seeks precarious shelter in trees. The one blessing they receive is pleasant weather. Luck also reaches the woodmen through them. If the goblins had not met with Bilbo and the dwarves, they would have arrived on time to meet the wargs and carry out a joint plan to kill or enslave the men and their families. "It looks almost as if the dwarves' journey is part of a larger plan that is shaping the destiny of Middle-earth" (Olsen 141). Indeed it is.

Gandalf does what he can to stop the wargs. But after goblins light fires under the trees, even he contemplates a defiant jump to his death and take as many of his opponents with him as he can. A moment before the wizard loses all hope, the Lord of the Eagles rescues him. Other Eagles come to aid of Bilbo and the dwarves. As servants of the Elder King, they lend grace-filled help several more times in the history Bilbo and Frodo recount in the Red Book.

Bilbo frantically clings to Dori's legs as the Eagles fly away. After two terrifying flights, the hobbit and his companions enjoy their first good meal in days. Bilbo sleeps deeper in this alien environment than he ever had in his plush bed at home.

Bilbo's dreams show his astonishing growth as an adventurous hobbit continues. The ones he had at home after he heard Thorin sing disturbed him. Then he had the vision of the imminent danger in the goblin cave. Now he dreams he is back home on the hunt for something he lost. Each dream has a message for him. The Vala, Irmo, Lord of Dreams, likely sent the one in the cave as a warning. He could have easily sent the others as to show Bilbo to himself. The hobbit no longer possesses the overwhelming need for safety and comfort that restricted his life before. Freed from this straitjacket, he gains the ability to fulfill his full potential. Olsen notes this shift:

> I think that in this dream, we can see a hint of how Bilbo's adventurous life is beginning to change him. Although his

Took side has gotten a great deal of exercise, his Baggins side has always been present, continually informing his perspective and his reactions. In this odd dream, we get the first suggestion that his Baggins side itself is being influenced and altered. He might seem as if he is not moved by his Wild surroundings, shutting his eyes to the sublimity and desiring only his safe and quiet world, but the dream suggests that his relationship with that domestic world is shifting. However much he may sometimes wish he could be magically whisked back to his home, he would not now be completely happy or satisfied if that wish somehow came true. Bilbo is seeking something that he cannot find at home in Bag-End, something that will only be found at the end of his journey. (139)

The next morning, the Eagles carry Gandalf, Bilbo and the dwarves away. The hobbit does not share the Eagle's joy of flight. The Company takes shelter in a small cave for the night. Gandalf mentions the role of luck in how far they have come. Anguish fills the hobbit and dwarves after the wizard announces he will leave them soon to attend to other matters.

Gandalf guides them to the shape-changer, Beorn. Their gruff host treats his guests to a richly laden table. Before they go to sleep, the wizard tells them not to go outside during the night. After Bilbo wakes and hears growls outside, he worries the bear-man will slay them. The next night, the hobbit dreams of myriad bears dancing around and again hears growls.

Beorn does not reappear until the morning. He says he went off to confirm the veracity of the tale he heard the first night. With the truth now known, he pledges his assistance in whatever way he can give it.

Luck continues to bless Bilbo, Gandalf, and the dwarves through Beorn. He gives them supplies for their journey and also loans them ponies. He says how unlikely they will find anything much to eat or drink in the forest without leaving the path. This he strictly warns them not to deviate from. The Company learns the seemingly disastrous detour through the mountains actually saved them from disaster. The shape-changer tells them not to travel the way they originally intended. The goblins now tread upon it, and it no longer leads anywhere good. He advises them instead to take a route several days away but little known. They could take advantage of its proximity to the goblin fortress because their enemies would not suspect they were near by.

The Company comes to the great and dark forest of Mirkwood. Gandalf reminds them he must now leave him, and they must leave the ponies. He points out Bilbo noticed Beorn shadowed their progress to guard the entire group. Before the wizard leaves, he twice admonishes them not to depart from the path.

As Bilbo and the dwarves begin their journey through Mirkwood, brief shafts of sunlight bless them. Their disappearance and the lack of any freshening wind gains the group's hearty hatred. As the Valar fashioned the sun, moon, and stars,

> [t]he light they produce is both a challenge to evil and a reminder of Ilúvatar's divine presence and guidance in the world.
>
> . . . Bilbo and his friends are not oppressed by the presence of nighttime in Mirkwood. . . . what presses down on them and chokes them . . . is the absence of any kind of light. . . . without light, they feel squeezed out of something vital to being. (Bell 112)

For days, the Company travels on with no sign of the end of this trial. They begin to worry whether their food supply will hold out. If Beorn had not warned them against drinking from the forest streams, they would from the first they come across.

Bilbo spies a boat on the other side, which after much labor, they bring over. All cross safely but for Bombur. He falls into the enchanted water after a deer startles him and into an enchanted sleep. The dwarves waste their arrows in a futile attempt to shoot other deer.

The sudden, unexpected sight of these particular animals signal the borderlands of faërie, a most perilous place for any mortal. Yet as it turns out, this is the place they must be to continue their journey. After they travel several more days, there is some light and air at last, as well as laughter and song. They do not like the sounds and move away from them.

Almost a week after the Company crossed the river, the dwarves draft Bilbo to climb a tree to see if he finds any sign of the wood's end. Sunlight and a fresh breeze reward the hobbit's struggle. But it is for naught. He sees nothing to encourage him they are almost through.

The next day, Balin reports he sees firelights ahead of them but off their path. After some debate, they make the fateful decision to do what they were repeatedly warned not to do. After several unwelcome attempts to make contact with Elves, Bilbo is left alone in the terrible darkness.

Magnificent

Bilbo falls into a light sleep, but grace alerts him to a gigantic spider about to put the finishing touches on the cocoon it wrapped him in. At the sight of Sting, it retreats long enough for the hobbit to get his legs free. He also continues to unwrap the cocoon of safety and comfort his Baggins side trapped him in all his adult life. After he goes on the attack, the spider does not flee from him fast enough.

Bilbo collapses after this great victory. Once he wakes, the sight of his dead adversary profoundly changes the hobbit's perception of himself. Just as in the goblin tunnels, he triumphs over his foe alone, in complete darkness, and without adequate food or rest. His Baggins side confronted its fears at the same time his Tookishness embraced the challenges before it. "This is the key moment in Bilbo's inner journey. Everything that came before was preparation for this instant, and everything that came after is the testing and using of this change . . ." (Shire Collective 163).

Fear still grips Bilbo, but he has radically changed his relationship with it. From the time he escapes from the goblins, it no longer dominates his life. Courage and sacrificial love for his friends replaces it.

The hobbit begins to search for his companions and laments they ever left the path. Grace points him in the right direction. He puts on his magic ring and finds the dwarves bound up in webs. Bilbo kills two spiders and then launches a grander assault. He mocks his foes in song and takes them on a merry chase. The enraged spiders spin web after web to capture their adversary. Luckily, in their haste, they do not construct them well. Bilbo easily escapes their traps in a way his Baggins side would have previously collapsed in terror just to imagine. He becomes fully alive as the adventurer Gandalf sought and Bilbo himself wished to be in his youth. As his enemies discover, these events help "sharpen the hobbit and hone him into something new and better: a weapon" (Bell 116). The spiders see Bilbo's sword but not its invisible wielder. He makes his way stealthily back to the cocooned dwarves.

Luckily, a spider left a thick web hanging down from a branch. Bilbo uses this as a rope, kills the guardspider, and frees Fili. Even with dwarf's aid, five of their companions remain trapped by the time the other spiders return. Bilbo wins frees from those in the tree and engages those on the ground. The hobbit realizes even with the valiant help of all the now freed dwarves, it is only a matter of time before fatigue becomes an enemy as well.

Bilbo chooses to tell his friends about his secret possession. He lays out his plan to draw off their adversaries. Some of the spiders chase his mocking voice; others almost overwhelm the dwarves as they flee. In the nick of time, Bilbo comes back. Just as the hobbit reaches the end of his strength, the spiders decide to retreat. The Ring-finder is now a power any evil should take notice of and properly fear. Decades later, the mother of these creatures also discovers what formidable enemies hobbits make.

Curiosity about Bilbo's ring distracts the dwarves from the lingering weakness of their ordeal. Their stomachs have shrunk, but their admiration and gratitude for their formerly unwanted companion greatly expands.

After Elves capture the dwarves, Bilbo follows invisibly behind. As they come to the Elvenking's fortress, fear threatens to smother the hobbit. At the last moment, loyalty to his friends gives him the strength to free himself long enough to slip in. Once inside, terror of discovery so rules him, he remains invisible and barely closes his eyes. At the same time, Bilbo considers this the most boring he has spent so far. But this is actually the best place for him and the Ring right now.

Wretchedness fills Bilbo even more than the food he must steal to survive. Olsen notes, "The experience has given him a whole new appreciation of the life that he had held without truly valuing it. His desire to return to his hobbit-hole is no longer simply escapism, an attempt to avoid or deny the harsh new reality surrounding him. Now, he recognizes Bag-End for what it really is: a paradise of warmth, light, rest, peace, and satisfaction" (178-179).

To pass the time, Bilbo acquaints himself with the layout of the palace and the schedule of the guards. In this way, he discovers the location of his imprisoned friends. The hobbit's presence strengthens Thorin's wavering resolve not to tell the Elves anything. He fully expects Bilbo to come up with some plan, so they can continue their journey. Long gone is the dwarves' misgivings about him; now he has their complete confidence.

Bilbo is not so serene about the chances of success himself. He does not like to be in charge, but he accepts the reality he is. He has no idea how he will rescue his friends until he happens to discover an alternate exit from the stronghold. The king's cellars could be accessed by trapdoors through which empty barrels were dumped into the river. As the hobbit observes this, the seed of a bold plan begins to grow. "Luck of an unusual kind" aids him (*Hobbit* 219). He hears talk of a great feast. After the king's butler and chief of guards get drunk and fall unconscious, Bilbo seizes his golden opportunity to grab the keys and free the dwarves. They reject his audacious escape plan out of hand. The hobbit confronts them with the only other alternative: return to their cells until they come up with some other idea that better suits them.

Bilbo returns the keys to the sleeping guard. This act of kindness provides an insulating effect against the Ring he has worn non-stop. No sooner has he finished loading the dwarves into the barrels, Elves come to put them into the water.

Bilbo then sees the one flaw in his plan. How is he to escape himself? He catches the final barrel and clings invisibly to the outside, as it plunges into the water. The hobbit tries and fails to get to the top of it. What seems bad luck turns out providential after the ceiling slopes sharply downward. If Bilbo was on top, he would be crushed. His luck holds as he floats down the river. He takes advantage of a brief time of stability to climb out of the cold water and on the top of his barrel.

Grace blesses the entire Company after they come to the tie-up point. The raftmen count the barrels, tie them up, and leave. As it is already after dark, they do not inspect the barrels, as they normally would. Sarah Arthur points out, "Bilbo is more than merely lucky; he's in good hands" (128).

In the morning, Bilbo hears from the raftmen of another instance of luck. The willful disobedience to leave the path is actually the best thing they could have done. As wretched as their time in the Elvenking's palace was, it was meant to happen to bring them to this place by the only possible route. Michael Martinez notes, "Hence, the white stag could also be interpreted as a sign of 'divine intervention', where a higher power sets into motion events that inevitably lead to the Dwarves' being captured so that they could successfully complete their journey to Erebor" ("White Stag").

Once alone again, Bilbo uncovers Thorin's barrel and enlists the dwarf's aid to free the others. The hobbit and three of the dwarves surprise the guards at the shore. The people of Lake-town embrace them all with open arms. Two weeks later, Thorin announces his intention to continue on to the Mountain and confront Smaug.

After several days, Bilbo and his companions reach the Desolation of the Dragon. As winter nears, they begin their search for the secret back door entrance. At last, the hobbit finds a path otherwise invisible unless one was right on top of it. With Kili and Fili, he follows it and finally discovers the hidden door.

The next morning, while the dwarves search for how to open the door, a low-spirited Bilbo spends his time in thought. He has a grand view of the surrounding area: Mirkwood, the Misty Mountains, and even further, the Shire he sees only in his heart and continues to long for. This is precisely where Ilúvatar wants him.

The following day, Bilbo has a strong sense some important event is about to happen. Olsen notes the essentialness of the hobbit at this particular moment:

> It is Bilbo, of course, who pays attention to the runes and respects what they say. He is the one waiting patiently by the grey stone, and since he has been thinking about the moon-letters, he is also the one who notices the thrush cracking snails against the side of the rock and realizes the prophecy is being fulfilled. . . . when the dwarves are groaning in disappointment as the sun runs into the bank of clouds on the horizon, Bilbo is the one who keeps up his hope, continuing to stand almost motionless next to the stone. Thorin, who only approaches the rock-face when Bilbo calls

for him, would not even have thought to try the key . . . in the miraculous key-hole if it weren't for the hobbit. The other occasions in which Bilbo has saved the day might have been a little more action-packed, but none are more important than this one. (203)

Without knowing it, the hobbit and dwarves come on Durin's Day to witness a stab of sunlight at the precise moment it pinpoints the way into the Mountain. All their delays, round-about paths, and seeming disasters have brought them to this providentially timed instant.

As a door opens into great blackness, the dwarves freeze in fear. They and Bilbo are now opposite of where they were at the beginning. Then the dwarves sang of the adventure to come, and the hobbit collapsed in terror. Now Bilbo allows the frightened Thorin to volunteer him to investigate whether Smaug is in residence. After all, the dwarf says, this is the whole point why Bilbo is here. What a splendid opportunity for him to take advantage of his "good luck far exceeding the usual allowance" (*Hobbit* 261). This rather annoys the hobbit, but he is now the adventurous one and agrees to enter.

Bilbo would not have recognized himself had he glimpsed this future self. The Baggins side of him wishes he was home. What use are dragon-hoards to him? Fear stops him in his tracks. He knows without a doubt Smaug is at home. But Bilbo has changed too much to allow fear to master him for long. He, who was once frightened by his imagination of a cook-fire being dragon-fire, now walks straight toward a real dragon. All the challenges the hobbit courageously overcomes show to him who he was always meant to be, who Gandalf intuited he was, and who Ilúvatar sees perfectly. He continues to wage this spiritual warfare throughout his adventure. His heroism is consistently an internal, willed choice.

Bilbo invisibly enters Smaug's lair while the dragon sleeps. The awesome spectacle of so many treasures in one place fills the hobbit with the dwarven desire for such things. He steps inside, nearly against his own choice, and steals a cup. But Smaug's unsettling dream about a pint-sized warrior shows Bilbo has grown far beyond mere burglar.

The dragon's enraged discovery of the theft cuts short the excitement of the dwarves. Smaug flies out his front door in search of the criminal. Bilbo tells his companions they must enter the tunnel before the dragon discovers them. The worm spends the night in a futile search and then returns to his lair.

The coming of day lessens the dwarves' fear of the dragon. They remain, however, at a loss as to how to defeat him. Bilbo volunteers to return to Smaug, who he hopes will be taking his afternoon siesta. He thinks he knows what to expect now and so feels no fear.

The hobbit discovers the dragon's sleep is mere pretense, but he wrongly assumes his invisibility will keep him safe. Smaug smells and hears his guest and invites him to take more of the treasure. Bilbo refuses and states he only came to investigate the accuracy of the stories told about the dragon. He knows enough lore not to give his true name after the worm asks for it. Instead he enjoys himself as he teases his foe with all sorts of true but riddling nicknames.

During this time, Bilbo faces great peril, not only physically but spiritually as well. Even though Smaug cannot see the hobbit's body, he still reaches into his heart and soul. These he tries to infect with suspicion and distrust of the dwarves. Bilbo feels a terrible urge to take off his ring and tell Smaug everything anytime the dragon looks unknowingly in his direction. While the hobbit resists this, he does begin to wonder about the veracity of the promise the dwarves made to share the amassed wealth equally with him. And, even if they do keep their word, how in the world will he ever transport it home without a tremendous amount of bother? Despite Smaug's verbal assaults, Bilbo remains loyal to his companions and their friendship. He tells the dragon the real goal of the dwarves is to avenge themselves on him for all their losses. Smaug scorn this as utterly ridiculous to attempt. He regales Bilbo with news of his past victories against men and dwarves.

Bilbo exploits the dragon's pride to trick him to reveal his one vulnerable spot. "Once again, Gandalf is proven wise for having foreseen that a simple hobbit could succeed using cleverness whereas a mighty warrior would have likely failed using might" (Gardner and Phillips 36).

The hobbit's own pride grows so much he taunts Smaug at the end and barely escapes with his life. After the dragon's wrath burns his feet, Bilbo recognizes his folly and turns from it. The dwarves tend to his injuries and attempt to bolster his spirits. They want to hear everything that happened. The hobbit fears he spoke too freely and put the Lake-men in peril. Balin tries to comfort his friend and speaks of "a mercy and a blessing" that may still come from Bilbo's discovery of Smaug's weak spot (*Hobbit* 281).

The hobbit has a strong intuition the dragon will attack their area again and insists they all come back inside for protection. The dwarves do so, but they do not close the door completely.

Bilbo tells his companions of Smaug's insinuations they were not going to keep up their end of the deal. The dwarves confirm they had not thought of how to transport the stolen wealth. However, they insist not only will the hobbit get his promised share, they will help him get it home.

Luck continues to shield Bilbo and the dwarves. The hobbit's sense of foreboding rises to such a degree he knows the precise moment Smaug is near. Barely in time do the dwarves heed the Ring-finder's pleas to close the door and save themselves from the dragon's wrath.

After Smaug fails to find his enemies, he flies off to avenge himself on Lake-town. The following silence is even worse than the terrible racket he made. Bilbo and the dwarves endure their entombment until some try the impossible task of opening the door again. As despair eats away his companions, "Bilbo felt a strange lightening of his heart . . ." (*Hobbit* 288). It knows of Smaug's death, but his conscious mind does not.

In an earlier draft of the tale, Tolkien toyed with an extraordinary idea. After Smaug returns from an unsuccessful bid to destroy Lake-town, Bilbo would be the dragon-slayer. Upon the gush of blood that issues forth from the great worm, the hobbit floats away in a bowl. John Rateliff notes:

It would mark the apotheosis of little Bilbo, *the* Hobbit, who has passed in the course of the story from 'fat little fellow bobbing on the mat' to reluctant traveller very much out of his depth, to effective warrior (and slayer of dozens of giant spiders), highly competent burglar (who evades the wood-elves in their own halls for weeks, if not months), resourceful lucky number (whose plan gets all his companions out of their dungeons and safely away back on their adventure), to here being the only one who dares to do a deed that no hero or warrior could accomplish. (374; emphasis in original)

But then Tolkien discovered the truth. Bilbo's mystical connection to what happens out in the world of men, as well as hobbit wisdom, strengthen his belief all is not lost. This gives him a great tactical advantage over his companions, who only feel the weight of doom suffocate them. He says he will return to Smaug's lair for the third time to see if the dragon is there or not.

This time the dwarves accompany Bilbo. After a while, the path ends without warning. The hobbit tumbles into the treasury room. Fear tries to strangle him. Around its grip, he cries out a challenge to Smaug. "[H]e would rather die in the light, throwing insults and defiance at his enemy, than cower in the dark. Bilbo is the stinging fly once again" (Olsen 227).

But the dragon is not there. The hobbit takes a torch and begins to look around. The dwarves linger on the threshold, still too afraid to enter. A pale light draws Bilbo ever on. It grows brighter, and finally he beholds it: the Arkenstone. The beauty of the gem causes him to briefly fall back into dragon-sickness. As the hobbit again lives up to his assigned job title, the precise wording of this indicates it happens almost independent of his own will: "Suddenly Bilbo's arm went towards it drawn by its enchantment" (*Hobbit* 291). He realizes he will eventually have to reveal what he took. He tries to justify taking it by reminding himself Thorin explicitly told him he could choose his own share. His conscience, however, tells him the dwarf did not mean this particular gem. Even so, the discovery of the priceless jewel by Bilbo in particular reveals another reason Ilúvatar guided Gandalf to choose the hobbit for this adventure.

Once the dwarves finally enter the chamber, their hearts flame up. They forget their fear and begin to gorge themselves on the treasures. Thorin seeks for the Arkenstone. He freely gives Bilbo the unimaginably wealthy gift of a *mithril* coat. Like the Ring and the Arkenstone, this gift comes to the hobbit for the purpose of giving it away.

Dragon-sickness consumes the dwarves, but such lust has already worn off for Bilbo. He longs once more for simpler pleasures. At long last, they agree not to press their luck any further with Smaug's whereabouts still unknown and leave the area.

The ancient raven Roäc proclaims the glad tidings of Smaug's death. He also tells them Men and Elves march toward the now unguarded hoard. The dwarves retreat and begin to fortify the mountain. Bilbo accompanies them, but he just wants everything over with.

Several days later, Bard comes to parley. The man seeks a portion of Smaug's wealth to succor those now homeless. Thorin refuses. Avarice holds his heart in a vise and eclipses his reason.

After days without battle and contending with the fear someone will discover his theft of the Arkenstone, Bilbo is heartily sick of everything. The priceless gem has a hold on the hobbit, but he desires peace more. He knows the stone is not truly his. If he kept it, he would be no better than Smaug. It came into his hands for another purpose. On some level Bilbo understands this. This scenario plays itself once more decades later, as he relinquishes the Ring. Both surrenders, difficult as they are, show the only cure for dragon-sickness. They also demonstrate rightful stewardship over gifts only lent for a time.

Bilbo goes to where Bombur stands on watch. The dwarf gratefully accepts the hobbit's offer to take his turn. Bilbo, however, has no intention to simply stand guard. He puts on his magic ring and steals away to the opposing camp.

On the way, the Elves capture Bilbo. Quite assertively, he asks they bring him to Bard and the Elvenking. He drops two bombshells. Another army of dwarves approaches them. Bard is openly suspicious of the hobbit's intentions, but Bilbo does not betray his friends with this secret visit. He bridges both sides to benefit both. He then reveals his second and far greater surprise. He gives the astounded man and Elf the Arkenstone in an "act of quiet heroism" (Olsen 265). Though it is a wrench to part with, he hopes it may bring peace before a deadly and needless conflict starts. His heart lies in the warm land of the living, not with treasure that turned Thorin's heart into such a cold, dead place. Only after Bard questions Bilbo as to how he came to possess such a priceless object does the hobbit become uncomfortable and admit the gem is not exactly his. "Yet it is in this very discomfort Bilbo's nobility . . . emerges. It is, in a strange way, proof of his sincerity; smoother speech might have sounded too glib" (Ang 57).

The Elvenking recognizes Bilbo's greatness, but he does not know if Thorin will. He counsels the hobbit to stay with him where his welcome is assured. The Elven way of life more naturally attracts Bilbo's heart, but he values loyalty to his friends and remaining true to his word to Bombur above all else. On the way out, Gandalf congratulates him and cheers him up. Bilbo returns to the mountain, wakes Bombur, and sleeps peacefully with the knowledge he did the right thing.

The next morning Bard, the Elvenking, and Gandalf come to parley with Thorin. As they reveal the Arkenstone, wonder and rage consume the dwarf. After Bilbo courageously confesses what he did, only Gandalf's timely intervention prevents the hobbit's murder. Some of the other dwarves feel compassion for Bilbo. Before the Ring-finder departs, he speaks of the possibility they may still salvage their torn bond. Richard Purtill notes:

> The kind of courage exhibited by Bilbo in this incident is not the usual heroism of the folktales. He has to make a lonely moral decision as to rights and wrongs in a complex situation, devise a plan with no help or support from those who should be his friends, and carry it out alone. His return to face the rage of the Dwarves shows another kind of courage, exhibiting a sense of honor and obligation. . . . For all his pretense sometimes to be 'businesslike' and 'sensible',

friendship is not a business matter for Bilbo: for him friendship involves giving even if you do not receive. The true word of what he calls friendship is love. . . . (66)

Adventure's End

Bilbo does not receive his exact wish in surrendering the Arkenstone to avoid a battle. His action, however, delays its onset and gives time for the fight to become an eucatastrophic one rather than catastrophic. Just as the dwarves are about to engage their foes, the true enemies of them all come. Rather than fight against each other, dwarves, Elves, and men unite against the goblins and wargs.

Bilbo does not take part in the battle. He puts on his ring and disappears. He looks unhappily at the terrible slaughter on both sides from the vantage point of Ravenhill where the Elves are. He thinks if it appears their enemies will win, he would rather fight with the Elven forces. He witnesses the eucatastrophic arrival of the Eagles before a stone knocks him out.

Bilbo does not wake until the battle is over and won, thanks to Beorn's timely intervention. Gandalf takes the hobbit to Thorin's deathbed to hear the dwarf's last words. Thorin lets Bilbo know he now realizes where true treasure lays. It is no less than the hobbit way of life. Stratford Caldecott notes, "Not only is Bilbo himself transformed by his adventures, but he also becomes a transformative influence on others, a catalyst for spiritual growth" (38). Though the dwarf's passing fills the hobbit with grief, he recognizes the grace they both receive to part as friends.

Dain wishes to give Bilbo a greater amount of Smaug's treasury than anyone else. The hobbit's reply shows how free he is from dragon-sickness. He has peace those infected with this potentially fatal disease do not and is content with only a couple boxes. Bilbo says farewell to his dwarven companions with mutual invitations to renew their ties in the future.

Gandalf and Bilbo accompany Beorn and the Elves. The hobbit grants the king a necklace in embarrassed repayment for stealing so much food and drink. The Elf bestows upon Bilbo the titles of Magnificent and elf-friend and calls him blessed.

Bilbo and Gandalf winter at Beorn's house. As much as the hobbit wants to go home, he is also sorry he must leave. His Baggins side begins to return to the forefront with his adventures over.

Well into spring, Bilbo and Gandalf return to Rivendell. The hobbit hears the wizard and Elrond speak of the Necromancer's flight from Mirkwood. The Elf-lord does not think their enemy's downfall will come about anytime soon. Little does he or any but Ilúvatar know how this is already set in motion unknowingly by Bilbo.

The hobbit spontaneously composes a poem to celebrate at last the sight of home in the distance. Jill Delsigne notes how it commemorates the Road which lead him into the world of the epic and now leads him back to where he began:

> Bilbo's ability to write this poem embodies his capacity to respond to his experiences of evil not with despair, but with the hope that he can find happiness and peace back in the Shire. . . . Bilbo turns to poetry to express the complexity of the eucatastrophic emotion he feels. . . .
>
> . . . Bilbo uses the metaphor of a story to think about his life. Like Tolkien, he sees his own life as a story that will continue long after he is no longer part of it. ("Hobbits" II:102)

Gandalf is quite right Bilbo is a different person than the one who rushed out the door unprepared for adventure a lifetime ago. They come to Bag-End just in time to stop the end of the auction of the hobbit's homely goods. Other hobbits assumed an untimely death was the reason for Bilbo's disappearance without a trace. It takes a great deal of time and trouble to convince them such rumors are greatly exaggerated.

Those neighbors who are not convinced Bilbo lives even after they see him in the flesh are actually right. "The Bilbo Baggins we met at the beginning has in fact passed away. The Bilbo who was paralyzed by doubt and fear is no more. The hobbit who had no chance of surviving a perilous venture has indeed been killed by it - and someone new lives in his place" (Bell 233). One who tells the dwarves they can drop by any time, as opposed to the one who liked to have all his appointments planned out in advance. Spontaneity replaces control. Bilbo left his home without even a handkerchief.

He returns wealthy, not only materially but spiritually. "[T]his Hobbit, who didn't have a shred of poetry in him before setting out on his adventure, comes home with poetry in his soul" (Smith 152). The Tookish part of him sees he never returns to solely an unadventurous, predictable Baggins. He enjoys his pipe and reflects upon the sword and priceless coat of mail he now owns. His walks take him into contact with Elves. He is who he was always meant to be. Jane Chance notes, "Bilbo has progressed from the chronological maturity of a fifty-year-old 'grown up' . . . to the state of wonder and joy common to the child - and the Christian" (70). Anne Petty remarks, "He passes all the return obstacles and is relieved to be back in his comfortable, civilized hobbit hole; yet, there are elements of Faërie that cling to him and somewhat hamper his complete return to his old life" (267).

Years later, Gandalf and Balin come to visit Bilbo and talk about old times and catch the hobbit up on what happened after they parted. The wizard demonstrates he is quite aware of the hand Providence had in the hobbit's entire journey and how Bilbo himself was one of its instruments. What appeared as lucky happenstances were much more than that. Grant Sterling observes, "Real prophecies come from minds inspired by the timeless God with knowledge of what is to come. But perhaps Bilbo *is* truly lucky after all - lucky to have been chosen to play such a great part in a providential plan" (216; emphasis in original). "In the end, Bilbo chose the path less traveled, the Tookish path, and this indeed made all the difference - to Bilbo and to all of Middle-earth" (Bassham 17).

The Hobbit ends the way *The Lord of the Rings* does, with a hobbit at home and adventures done, at the least for some decades.

Farewell to the Shire

The spiritual and material gifts Bilbo received he passes on. They transform all of Middle-earth in time. Generations live in peace because Gandalf obeyed the prompting of his Creator to choose this particular hobbit as a participant in events only Ilúvatar foresaw.

> If Bilbo had not found the Ring, he would not have survived his own Quest, nor would it have been likely that he would have lived long enough to take Frodo as his Ward. In this sense . . . the Ring conspired in Its own destruction. For by prolonging Bilbo's life, It meant that he was able to raise up Frodo as his heir.
>
> . . .
>
> Also, we have a good many . . . hints of the way Bilbo raised Frodo: taking him on rambles about the Shire, teaching him Elven tongues and history, and there are hints that Bilbo took Frodo to meet Elves. We see that Bilbo is no longer a shy or timid hobbit, but that he rather revels in his own eccentricity, and seems to enjoy tweaking the noses of more 'hide-bound' hobbits. This too must have been a factor in Frodo's own less than conventional behavior. We also see the impact Bilbo has on the Shire: while he may not be 'respectable' he is popular. Everyone wants to be at his Party, and though there is much gossip, it's clear that the hobbits of his area are fond of him for his generosity and kindness. (Dreamflower)

These many positive aspects to Bilbo's journey do not entirely cancel out the toll the Ring takes on the hobbit. Judith Klinger notes:

> Separated from Sauron, the Ring seeks to reunite with him, and this primary purpose of achieving Oneness is at the bottom of all Its interactions with Its subsequent bearers. It seeks to merge with Its bearer, . . . to establish dependence

and obliterate any difference between them. . . . Its nature can therefore be likened to that of a parasite: It lends the bearer unnatural long life while draining his life energy. ("Fallacies" I:357)

Bilbo's taste for another adventure grows to the point he desires to retrace his steps from sixty years before. The Shire was a wonderful place to come back to, but he needs something more now. He makes plans to return to the only other place he really felt at rest: Rivendell.

On his eleventy-first birthday, Bilbo announces his great affection for his fellow hobbits and the importance of this particular birthday for Frodo. The old hobbit says farewell and makes an abrupt disappearance from his own party. The younger Baggins barely controls his amusement at the consternation of the other guests. At the same time his heart aches with love and loss.

Bilbo invisibly returns home to pick up the few belongings he will take with him. Unlike Sméagol who gained the Ring on his birthday through murder, its present Bearer relinquishes it on his. He plans to leave it for Frodo, but then he changes his mind.

Or has it changed for him.

Gandalf comes to see Bilbo before he leaves. The hobbit confesses the odd sensations he felt recently and thinks a never-ending vacation may help alleviate them. He notes Frodo offered to accompany him. But though the elder Baggins is ready to say good-bye to the Shire, he knows his beloved heir is not.

The wizard reminds Bilbo of their previously made arrangement for the hobbit to surrender the Ring before he leaves. The wrench to part with the precious object is far worse than with the Arkenstone. The struggle even goes so far as to threaten to sunder his decades-long friendship with Gandalf. The hobbit tells the wizard where he left it. To his surprise, he finds it instead in his pocket, as though he did not realize he put it there. He decides it should remain there after all and is upset Gandalf pesters him about it. This and hearing Bilbo call the Ring as Gollum did disturbs the wizard. He suspects the Ring "has some sort of lethal ability to ensnare its user" (Rutledge 53). Gandalf repeatedly insists the hobbit stick to his word and part with the perilous treasure. Just as stubbornly, Bilbo insists he will keep it and almost threatens the wizard with Sting. Gandalf nearly loses his patience with such nonsense. He says if Bilbo keeps it up, the hobbit will see the wizard's true power.

Bilbo has a vision of his friend who "seemed to grow tall and menacing; his shadow filled the little room" (*LotR* I:1, 33). After a silent confrontation of wills, Gandalf turns away first. Why a shadow? If this is truly "Gandalf the Grey uncloaked" (*LotR* I:1, 33), then would not one see a bright angelic light? But there is no mention of this. Possibly the shadow Bilbo sees is how Gandalf would appear as a Ring-lord. Others also appear in visions as tall beings while the Ring is at work in them before they shrink down to themselves: Frodo's vision of Galadriel as the Ring tempts her; Sam's two visions of his master, one in the Emyn Muil and one near the threshold of the Sammath Naur; and the gardener's own feeling of enlargement in the Tower of Cirith Ungol. A light shines only on Galadriel during her struggle. Sam's first vision mentions a cloud covering brightness. Frodo's transfiguration at the Fire shows a bright figure. Perhaps there is no light in Bilbo's vision of Gandalf because there would be no light left in the Maia if he claimed the Ring. Tolkien noted the wizard would be worse than Sauron as a Ring-lord (*Letters* 332-333).

Bilbo apologizes for his outburst and agrees it would be better if he was rid of the Ring. He tells of his curious perception it sometimes seems it watched him. At last, he heeds Gandalf's angelic counsel to leave it behind.

But the Ring still has its tendrils wrapped around the hobbit. He drops the envelope that contains it. Gandalf retrieves it before Bilbo can. The momentary hostility the hobbit feels as the wizard thwarts his repossession of the precious "[s]uddenly . . . gave way to a look of relief and a laugh" (*LotR* I:1, 34). If the Ring "suddenly" caused Bilbo to put it back into his pocket without even realizing it, now grace "suddenly" shows him what he will feel like without the Ring's terrible presence. The obsessive need to always have it on his person lifts from him. "And so ends the first eucatastrophic moment of *The Lord of the Rings*. It is a moment of great hope, often overshadowed by the darkness to follow, but should also be seen as instructive in the nature of grace in Middle Earth" (Ilverai).

Bilbo's song of the Road shows what an exciting time this is for him. He embarks again with dwarven companions. This time it is for an adventure he deliberately planned and longed for. Yet William Reynolds notes there is also the memory of danger of venturing forth and where the Road may lead:

> But [Bilbo] still experiences not only the typical hobbit reluctance to cut himself off from what is familiar but also a troublesome foreboding about what the future holds for one who has given up his power. All this the poem makes clear: while Bilbo can claim to be 'pursuing it with eager feet' . . . he repeats the poem slowly and quietly, pausing after its final verse, 'And whither then? I cannot say,' balancing within himself the new freedom to be gained against what may very well be lost. (12)

Frodo laments he was not back in time to say goodbye to his uncle. Gandalf tells him Bilbo intended to leave without any further ado.

> This scene to me epitomizes the strong tie between Frodo and Bilbo as well as their very real difference in temperament: Bilbo who often hides his concern about serious things behind a joke now prefers to disappear rather than having to face his nephew whom he loves; Frodo hoping that Bilbo's threat to leave was merely a joke and wishing he had said goodbye despite the pain in such an intimate exchange. It is this ability to feel for another person that will 'save' Frodo from the allure of the Ring, at least for a very long time. His ability to 'feel' for Bilbo, the Shire, and, perhaps most of all, Samwise will be his first line of defense against the lure of evil. (Child of the 7th Age)

The morning after the party, Frodo tells Gandalf he longs to reunite with his uncle and wishes he left with him.

Chosen

Some hobbits think Bilbo finally went insane and died. This perception of peculiar behavior attaches itself to Frodo also. He shows no grief for his uncle and continues the tradition of lavish birthday parties for him. The younger Baggins continues to cultivate his familiarity with the Elves and their language. He loves to take long walks either alone or with his favorite cousins, Merry and Pippin. Dan Hollingshead considers these "all windows into Frodo's character. His knowledge of the outside world was probably very incomplete; but if one knows the name of Elbereth, wouldn't they want to walk alone under the stars at night and wonder about the Star-Kindler, and the One who taught her the music?" (61). Trudy G. Shaw agrees:

> Bilbo had to go there and back again in order to reach the state he passes on to Frodo: a state in which he wanders alone under the starlight and converses with Elves. A state in which - although he wouldn't recognize the term - he's developing a spiritual life. And it's primarily a contemplative spiritual life, based not on what he does but on who he is . . . .
>
> Frodo's will always be an interior focus - necessary ultimately to confront the Ring, but present in his personality from the beginning. ("He lived")

Before Frodo reaches 50, the same restlessness for adventure fills him as it had Bilbo. He also contends with the same struggle with his Baggins and Tookish sides whether he will give into this longing or not. He gains news from Elves and dwarves he meets during his longer and longer walks. Rumors of a growing darkness reach his ears.

Frodo receives his chance for adventure, willing or not, after Gandalf returns after a long absence. The wizard has but one final test to prove his dark suspicions about Bilbo's magic ring. He tells Frodo he did not know how Gollum could have acquired a Ring of

Power and thought Bilbo's tale too fanciful to be accurate. For decades, he did not pursue the matter. The catalyst to finally find out was Bilbo's deeply troubling behavior on the night of the farewell party. Frodo wonders if his uncle will recover from the damage done by the Ring. Gandalf assures him he will, though he admits its poisonous effects will linger for a long time.

The wizard asks to see the Ring. As the hobbit surrenders it to his friend, "It felt suddenly very heavy, as if either it or Frodo himself was in some way reluctant for Gandalf to touch it" (*LotR* I:2, 48). To the hobbit's alarm, the hidden Maia promptly throws it into the little fire Frodo has going. After Gandalf returns it untouched, its Bearer discerns the verse Sauron inscribed on it long ago in his bid to overwhelm all the other Rings of Power. There is no longer any doubt as to what Bilbo found in the goblin tunnels.

Gandalf confirms the sinister rumors circulating around the Shire: an old evil threatens Middle-earth once more. Frodo laments the timing of this. The wizard agrees all those who must face perilous times wish they were not caught up in them. He then gives one of greatest pieces of wisdom to follow: "All we have to decide is what to do with the time that is given us" (*LotR* I:2, 50).

Gandalf paints a grim picture for all those who oppose Sauron. Their only hope lies in the fact the Enemy does not yet have the Ring. Frodo's active imagination fancies the Dark Lord reach out to grab it from him. Gandalf tells the hobbit of Sméagol's long and miserable life as Ring-bearer under the Misty Mountains.

Once Frodo learns Sméagol's secondary name is Gollum, disgust fills him to even think this murderous rogue is a hobbit. He is sure the creature devised the riddle-game for his own wicked purposes. Gandalf does not disagree, but he still holds out some hope for the miserable being's cure. The wizard says hatred dominates Sméagol-Gollum's wretched life, with the greatest focused on the Ring. Frodo does not understand how the creature could feel this way about his beloved possession. If true, why did he not abandon it? Gandalf says it is beyond Gollum's ability to choose this. It was the Ring which chose to separate itself from him. But then something neither it nor Sauron could have anticipated happened. The wizard calls Bilbo's arrival to casually pick it up the oddest thing to happen to it since it was forged. Gandalf notes another power used Sauron's desire to find the Ring for its own purposes. It was this which made sure Bilbo and no one else was there at that precise moment. The wizard makes clear the same power also appointed Frodo to play a role in the great drama of the Ring. Gandalf means this to hearten the hobbit. But Frodo finds no comfort, though he admits his friend's words are beyond his full comprehension.

To the hobbit's great alarm, he learns Gollum is responsible for Sauron's knowledge of who has the Ring and where this person lives. He wishes Bilbo took advantage of his opportunity to kill the loathsome creature. Gandalf places a different emphasis on pity than Frodo does. It saved Bilbo and Gollum. The wizard admonishes Frodo for his desire for the wretched being's death. No one sees all the possibilities the future may hold. Faint though the hope may be for Gollum's rehabilitation, it remains one of the possibilities death would cut off. The wizard says there is something the creature is yet to do because Bilbo showed pity. This is likely to have a great impact on Frodo and many others. These words the younger Baggins does not forget, even though he cannot understand yet why Gandalf advocates for Gollum.

Frodo wishes the Ring never came into Bilbo's life or his own. He wonders why Gandalf left him in possession of such a dangerous thing. The wizard reminds him he did not know its true identity until now. He asks the hobbit how he would do away with it. After Frodo offers a couple options, the wizard tells him to make an attempt. The hobbit's actions demonstrate how deeply the Ring has sunk its talons into him. Its seeming beauty enthralls him. He has no wish to harm it, even after all he heard. He tries to will himself to cast it back into his fireplace. He discovers it safely returned to his pocket. Frodo's failure does not surprise Gandalf. Judith Klinger notes:

> This unexpected division of intent and action perfectly reflects the Ring's most basic mode of operation. It is capable of imposing Its own purpose on the bearer while masquerading as a beautiful but inanimate artefact. What

Frodo has learned about the Ring's origin and potential renders him aware of the discrepancy between action and decision, and this awareness in turn becomes crucial for his ability to resist the Ring. But at this point in the story, Frodo perceives only a division between his 'effort of will' and his actual response, which he doesn't yet attribute to the Ring. As long as the Ring can mask Its activities, Frodo is vulnerable to It. ("Fallacies" I:357)

This second episode of a hobbit's struggle with the Ring "is a moment of discatastrophe, mirroring the first, and casting the entire quest in doubt. It reinforces the impossibility of the quest and the necessity for providential aid, while the first episode reveals the real chance of success and the seed of hope" (Ilverai).

Gandalf tells Frodo he could not compel him to give up his treasure without driving him mad.

Frodo desires to bring an end to the Ring. But after he hears only the fires in faraway Mordor can do this, he no longer wishes to be the one to do it. He does not consider himself cut out for such a dangerous undertaking. "Why was I chosen?" (*LotR* I:2, 60).

Gandalf replies he does not know, but he confirms the decision was deliberately made. "Despite this emphasis on fate, however, free will does play a significant part in Tolkien's novel. Frodo is perhaps the ideal Ring-bearer, as his strength of character enables him to accept his fated role, yet also to retain a sense of free will in the face of the powerful, corrupting influence of the Ring" (Gardner et al. 82).

The wizard vehemently rejects Frodo's plea to take the Ring in his stead. Twice he begs the hobbit not to entice him with its power. He knows he is not strong to withstand the test if he actually became a Ring-bearer. He pledges his support to its ordained Bearer. The decision to accept this appointment rests on the hobbit's shoulders and heart alone, but this assurance of aid makes Gandalf "the messenger of the actual grace bestowed upon the hobbit . . ." (Wagner, "Sacramentum," 84). The wizard brings up two important, recurring themes: "One is that there is a benevolent force at work that opposes the power of evil, and that everyone has a role to play in its grand design. The other is that individuals should not be forced to do anything - even to follow their roles in the grand scheme of things" (Pienciak 74).

As Frodo ponders his choice, his active imagination presents a fearful picture. The fireplace becomes Mount Doom and envelops his whole world until Gandalf's voice recalls him. He announces he will remain the Ring's guardian, whatever the cost to himself.

> Here is the first glimmering of his Chosen status . . . a free will accepting, not a challenge, but a Calling. Although he does not yet fully understand the impact of this decision for himself, he understands the importance, the need for it, *for others.*
>
> It is a moment of supreme faith. And trust. Trust freely given - not coerced - despite what may come of it. (Wagner, "Sacramentum" 82; emphasis in original)

Gandalf assures Frodo, while his intentions remain as pure as they begin, the Ring will not easily corrupt him. The hobbit discovers more and more he crosses a threshold here. All his life, what is good is pleasant, and what is bad is harmful and unpleasant. But in this larger world he now steps into, good sometimes causes pain and asks for sacrifices, and evil at whiles seems easier and more attractive. The hobbit desires the discovery of a worthier custodian. Until then, he accepts he must leave his homeland in order to remove the peril of the Ring's continued presence. Already he feels he will not return. A sudden desire to see Bilbo again overcomes Frodo and temporarily erases how afraid he feels.

Gandalf admits his amazement at the hobbit's response and remarks Bilbo did not err after he decided upon Frodo to inherit what he had. The wizard gives the younger Baggins an alias to use if any ask and tells him to take a companion. Gandalf himself selects the perfect one: the eavesdropping Sam. David Mills notes the gardener's wish for the right weather to work in is one of the examples of providential aid throughout the tale: "Because the weather is good, Sam can work in the garden and . . . sneak under the window and listen to Gandalf and Frodo's discussion. . . . he gets caught . . . , is ordered to go with Frodo, and because he goes with Frodo, and helps him in ways no one else could have . . . , the Ring is destroyed against all odds ("Writer").

". . . by leaving [the Ring] in Frodo's possession, Gandalf isn't trusting Frodo but the Power that chose him, and is allowing that Power to act. The hope without assurance that's explicit at the Council is implicit here" (Shaw, "Gifted").

On the Road

The thought of finding Bilbo again almost made Frodo run out the door, as prepared for his adventure as his uncle was for his. He does not know his decision to take Gandalf's counsel to seek out the house of Elrond will fulfill his fondest wish. But even though reunion remains a priority, it does not prod him to leave soon. The newly christened Ring-bearer wants to enjoy every minute he has left in his homeland. He determines to begin his exile on his birthday. He sells Bag End to Lobelia and encourages the little-believed rumor it is because he needs the money.

Gandalf leaves the Shire with a pledge to return by Frodo's birthday. But he does not, nor does he the day after. Frodo leaves for Crickhollow with Sam and Pippin without knowing the reason for his friend's troubling delay.

> And so, whether he wishes it or not, Frodo is cast out onto the Road, forced to embark on a pilgrimage that he has long desired to take, but would never have had the courage or resolve to begin. But it will take him some time to really leave the Shire behind, to learn to think of himself as a true sojourner in a world that does not belong to him and that cannot, in any case, promise final rest. For the lesson that the journey is to teach us is not simply that it is good to go on pilgrimages, but that we are pilgrims. . . . The Bilbo we meet at the beginning of *The Lord of the Rings* has learned this lesson in part. It will be left to Frodo to learn it in full. (Markos 26)

"Frodo begins the Quest with humility, trust, realism, discernment, detachment, openness, faith, hope, and love" (Shaw, "Gifted"). Grace blesses him from beginning to end. Just before the hobbit leaves, he happens to hear the Gaffer talk to someone about his whereabouts. He does not know why he feels comforted the mysterious caller does not go further than Number 3. He attributes it to having more than enough of nosy neighbors and chooses not to investigate further. He does not know whether this is a good idea or not, but more than darkness shelters him from the chilling truth a Ringwraith came to call. The Ring-bearer leaves Hobbiton with Pippin and Sam without knowing if he will ever return.

The next morning, Frodo sings almost word for word the same song Bilbo had 17 years previously. "Bilbo bequeaths the Road poem, the burden of the Ring, and a way of alleviating the effect of evil by writing original poetry to Frodo. . . . Throughout [Frodo's] adventures, he will find his own voice and write his own poems in response to the evil he faces and from his perspective, his failure to resist that evil" (Delsigne II:103). The one change the Ring-bearer makes is while Bilbo's feet were excited to set out, his are tired. William Reynolds notes, "Frodo neither designed nor built the Road. He knows neither its beginning nor its end. But . . . he trusts the power that made the Road and permits himself to be swept off . . ." (12).

Frodo's return to Buckland is a study in opposites: ". . .what looks backward is really forward; what looks like regression is progress; what looks like a return to comfortable, familiar surrounding is actually a springboard into the uncomfortable, perilous wilderness" (mark12_30).

On the way to Crickhollow, Sam hears someone behind them. A strong intuition it is not the hoped-for Gandalf prompts Frodo to warn his friends to hide. The Ring-bearer does not get under cover himself until the last moment. Two things war within him: the necessity to do so and "curiosity or some other feeling" about who comes (*LotR* 1:3, 73).

Frodo's spiritual warfare against the Ring begins here. He watches a horseman draw near to his hiding place and has the unsettling experience of hearing someone sniff around particularly for him. The Ring tries to use Frodo's terror of discovery to compel him to put it on, and so announce itself to the Black Rider. Despite all Gandalf's warnings not to do this, such precautions do not make sense anymore in the face of this danger. But before the fell object can completely ensnare its Bearer, the Rider moves off and ruins its purpose.

After dark, the Black Rider comes upon them again. The compulsion to put on the Ring assaults Frodo so strongly his hand moves toward it almost independent of his own will. The only thing that keeps it from swallowing him whole is the unusual appearance of a passing company of High Elves. Their hymns to Elbereth frighten off the Rider and break the Ring's hold.

Gildor hails the Ring-bearer by name. He calls him Elf-friend after he hears Frodo speak in the Elven language. The Elves take the hobbits into their protection for the night after Pippin tells them of the pursuit by the Black Rider.

After Pippin and Sam fall asleep, Frodo speaks long to Gildor. He say he did not expect danger so soon. The Elf tells him the Shire does not belong solely to the hobbits. They live in blissful, willed, and protected ignorance of the evil outside their boundaries. But it will not remain this way forever. Hannah Eagleson notes:

> This is an especially moving and powerful thing for Frodo to hear at this moment. Ever since Gandalf told Frodo the story of the Ring, it has been dawning on Frodo that the comfortable life most Hobbits know, enclosed by the Shire and with little interaction with those outside, is not possible to maintain. The wide world is interrupting the quiet world of the Shire, and Frodo at least has to take notice. Gildor's words are a reminder that things must change and that the world of the Shire, which seems so settled and permanent, has been different in the past and will be different again. (*Wisdom:* FOTR 18)

Gildor does not wish to talk about the dangers that beset Frodo and his companions in any great detail because the Elf does not want to scare the hobbit off his appointed path. In an earlier draft of the tale, the Elf-lord makes a profound observation about the division within the Ring-bearer: ". . .the half that is plain hobbit will suffer much I fear from being forced to follow the other half which is worthy of the strange fate, until it too becomes worthy. . . . For that must be the purpose of your fate. . . . The hobbit half that loves the Shire is not to be despised but it has to be trained . . ." (*Return of the Shadow* 281).

Gildor senses it is not a coincidence he and his company met up with Frodo. But as he does not know the reason why, he remains frustratingly vague after the hobbit presses for more information about the Black Riders. The Elf feels in his heart the Ring-bearer will learn all too well who the Riders are and calls upon the Star-Kindler to guard him.

The next morning, what little Gildor said is enough to make Frodo reconsider his decision to take anyone with him. The Ring-bearer asks Sam if he still wishes to leave their homeland, with his dream to meet Elves already achieved. The gardener surprises his master with uncommon insight. He says he knows their Road will be a black one. This does not hold him back from renewing his commitment to stay upon it.

Frodo, Sam, and Pippin travel on until water stops them momentarily. By a lucky chance, the gardener takes the opportunity to look back up a steep bank. He spies a horse and its rider at the top. The hobbits barely have time to hide themselves. They travel several more miles before they take a break for lunch. They discover the Elves filled their water bottles with a refreshing gift. This drives all fear from them and fills them with mirth and song once more.

At least until two terrible cries come upon the wind.

Refuge

After Frodo and his companions reach Farmer Maggot's homestead, the Ring-bearer faces fear of another kind. This was his favorite place as a lad to steal mushrooms. The horrifying memory of the dogs as they ran him off the last time still haunts him decades later.

Maggot calls the hobbits into his home. He regales them with the report of a mysterious character he met earlier that day who inquired about Baggins. The farmer wonders if the stranger meant Bilbo. He realizes meeting Frodo, so soon after the man left, is no chance encounter.

After the hobbits cross the Brandywine into Buckland, Sam again responds to the intuition to look back and chances to see the Rider behind them on the opposite shore. The Ring-bearer and his friends hurry away.

Crickhollow provides a welcome refuge, but Frodo knows it is no true haven. With pursuit close behind him, he cannot long afford to tarry but must continue to flee. He will never be at home anywhere in the Shire again.

Frodo thinks only Sam knows of his intention to leave. He dreads how he will say farewell to his beloved cousins. Instead he passes through wonder, astonishment, and stupefaction to hear they are already privy to the Ring's existence and the plan to depart with it. Sam tells Frodo twice to take Gandalf's and Gildor's advice to take companions with him. Merry speaks beautiful words about the great power of love and friendship which binds the hobbits together. Despite their terrible fear of what lies ahead, they plan to stick to his side to counter the evil of the Ring. Notwithstanding all the dangers which already beset them, Frodo feels great delight.

"To the Ancients," C. S. Lewis wrote, "Friendship seemed the happiest and most fully human of all loves; the crown of life and the school of virtue" (*Loves* 87). Louis Markos notes, "It is precisely this spirit of unswerving loyalty and devotion, this binding together of separate lives and wills, that gives the Hobbits their staying power

- that makes them a fellowship, even when they are apart" (108). Stratford Caldecott concurs:

> . . . it all starts with friendship - the love of Bilbo for Frodo
> . . . ; Frodo's love for his fellow hobbits, which leads him to
> accept the need to leave the Shire for its own protection;
> and the love for Frodo, which causes Sam, Merry, and
> Pippin to stay by his side 'through thick and thin.' It is
> friendship - a love of the other for his own sake - that holds
> them together in the face of the challenges and trials that
> make them grow as people. By fighting together against
> great evils, they become capable of recognizing and standing
> up against the lesser evils and small corruptions of everyday
> life. (168)

Frodo asks how soon they can leave. Merry says he has already gathered much of what they will need. The Ring-bearer wonders whether he should wait one more day for Gandalf, but Merry says Buckland cannot keep the Riders away. Frodo decides to escape through the Old Forest despite all the dark rumors that surround it.

Throughout the Quest, prophetic dreams or visions visit the Ring-bearer. The first one comes here and places him somewhere where he is above trees but afraid sniffing beings below will find him. He hears and smells the Sea and comes upon a solitary tower. This sound visited him many times in the past while he slept, but he has never seen it. It foreshadows the blessing to come for the sacrifice of his entire self to the Quest Ilúvatar chose him for. Though Tolkien never calls the Ring-bearer's prescient dreams a sign Frodo has second sight, he does manifest this gift. The sniffing he hears is likely a glimpse of Gollum who comes near the night Frodo and his companions spend in the trees after they meet Haldir.

In the morning, Frodo, Sam, Merry, and Pippin enter the forbidding forest. Jane Chance observes:

In the first book Frodo comes to understand evil as external and physical through the descent into the Old Forest. . . . Both Old Man Willow and the barrow-wights represent the natural process of death caused, in Christian terms, by the Fall of Man.

. . .

Frodo learns . . . the presence of mutability, change, and death in the world is natural and continually repaired by growth and new life. In the second book [of *FOTR*] he learns through a parallel descent into the Mines of Moria that the spiritual form of death represented by sin stems from within the individual but is redeemed by the 'new life' of wisdom and virtue counseled by Galadriel. . . . (155, 156-157)

Frodo attempts to alleviate the oppressive atmosphere with a song. He trails off before the end after the trees show their displeasure. They see the hobbits as hostile threats and deal with them as such. Tom Shippey makes note of the profundity of the Ring-bearer's song:

. . . the 'shadowed land' is life, life's delusions of despair are the 'woods', despair will end in some vision of cosmic order which can only be hinted at in stars or 'sun'. What does Frodo mean by the repeated contrasts of setting/rising, west/east, day's end/day begun? They can hardly avoid suggesting death and life; in that case his song says there can be no defeat - even if the wanderers die in the dark world, the real Old Forest, they will in death break through to sunlight and out of a hampering shade. (*Road* 190)

Merry points out the direction of the Withywindle and says they must avoid it. Yet, as the hobbits travel on, they discover the path toward it is the route they are forced to take. No other opens for them. The hobbits travel a while longer until three of them surrender to a compulsion to sleep. Sam is the only one who withstands the spell Old Man Willow weaves. The gardener rescues his master after the malicious tree attempts to drown him.

Frodo and Sam make a frantic and near-disastrous attempt to free Merry and Pippin from inside the tree. After this fails, the Ring-bearer runs away in a blind panic. He has no idea if anyone of good will hear his desperate cries for help.

Someone does hear. The hobbits are not drawn this way through the Forest just by malevolent wills. Frodo draws to his cousins the only enfleshed being who can save them.   Who or what Tom Bombadil is remains one of Middle-earth's great mysteries. Perhaps all anyone need know is his power, great and lightly held, is the precise spiritual and physical aid the hobbits need. He orders Old Man Willow to release Merry and Pippin from prison and then calls them all to the home he shares with Goldberry.

Frodo's encounter with the River-daughter highlights the hobbit's sensitivity to the realm of the Ainur and his spiritual kinship with Elves. Her blessed presence and song so deeply moves the Ring-bearer, it inspires him to sing his own small tribute to her. Hannah Eagleson remarks Frodo's response "has wonder in it as well as a form of reverence - here is a being of admiration, a being different from [himself] . . ." (*Wisdom: FOTR* 37). Goldberry recognizes in turn the unique ways grace shines from him.

After Tom and Goldberry treat the hobbits to a feast, Frodo asks whether his cry brought him or was he there by happenstance? Tom replies it was the latter, but in such a way he means it actually played no part at all. He was nearby for something entirely different. His denial of the element of chance brings to light once more the providential timing of events that favors the success of the Quest.

In this blessed refuge, "under the influence of love and grace poured out in the shape of bread and meat and ale and downy soft beds, Frodo, Sam, Pippin, and Merry forgot their fears and found new strength for their journey" (Bruner and Ware 35).

Frodo has more dreams, or visions, here. The first one he receives is of Gandalf's escape from Orthanc, though he does not realize this until the wizard recounts the event at the Council of Elrond.

The hobbits spend a rainy day wrapped up in the enchantment of Tom's voice. He regales them with story after story of the grand history of their world. These are but a few of the brightly colored threads within a thickly woven tapestry. Not all of it is easy to hear, but the spell of this master storyteller enraptures his audience so completely Frodo's perception of time alters. He feels no need to eat or rest.

After Tom asks the hobbits about themselves, the Ring-bearer reveals more of his inner thoughts than he shared with anyone. Tom expresses his desire to see the Ring. Frodo previously hesitated to give it to Gandalf, a beloved and trusted friend. To his amazement, he gives it to Bombadil, a stranger, with no hesitation at all. If Tom and Goldberry are Maiar, they could be of greater power than Gandalf, and Frodo's soul recognizes and responds to this.

Tom demonstrates his power over the Ring. To the wonder of the hobbits, he does not vanish while he wears it. Rather, he makes it disappear while he plays with it. After Frodo gets it back, he wonders if their host played a trick on him. An undefined "something" makes him put it on. This betrayal of Frodo by the Ring is so subtle, he does not even realize it. Terrible, overt compulsion he can recognize and resist. This slips straight past his defenses without his conscious knowledge or desire. Once it holds him in its grip, it leads him away.

Merry's shock at Frodo's sudden disappearance proves the Ring is true. The Bearer pretends pleasure at his cousin's reaction, but he cannot quite manage it. He violated Gandalf's warning not to wear it, and he knows it. But even though he is invisible to his fellow hobbits, he is not to Tom. For all of Bombadil's frivolous treatment of the Ring, he is well aware of its evil. He tells Frodo to sit back down and take it off.

Tom teaches the hobbits a song to summon him if danger presses too close after they leave him.

That night, Frodo has another mystical experience. He catches a glimpse of the Undying Lands where he goes after his sojourn in Middle-earth. This and other visions are gifts to him, likely from the Vala Irmo, to console and strengthen him. Verlyn

Flieger observes, "Frodo travels in his dreams deeper and farther than any of the others was ever allowed to go" (*Question* 167).

> Besides Frodo's statement that he doesn't know if he was dreaming or in some other state of awareness, there's another aspect of this . . . that tells us the vision was beyond what he could put into words. . . . '. . . a song that seemed to come like a pale light . . .'
>
> Is it a song that's seen as a light, or light that's heard as a song? Or something else entirely? The incongruent reference to two different senses implies, I believe, that what Frodo is experiencing isn't something that can be captured by any one of our physical senses. . . . what he comes up with is a combination of hearing and sight, as if during this experience they became a single sense - a much richer sense than either of them taken alone. (Shaw, "in dreams")

The hobbits say farewell to Tom and Goldberry. The air itself heartens their spirits to eagerly continue on their Road.

Amidst the Barrow-downs, the hobbits enjoy a hearty meal in the warm sun. After some hours, they wake from a nap they did not consciously decide to take and discover themselves surrounded by fog. After Frodo passes between two standing stones, his pony gets spooked and throws him. He calls for his friends, hears their frantic cries for help, but he cannot reach them.

Frodo wakes inside a barrow. Though terror paralyzes him, grace reaches out to once more to rouse his courage. He "found himself" thinking of Bilbo and "found himself" tighten for battle (*LotR* 1:8, 137). He sees his three companions unconscious and perhaps dead. He hears a chilling voice begin a spell and sees an arm reach near Sam.

A terrible temptation to put on the Ring and flee this horrible place before the wight binds him too to its wicked spell take holds of Frodo. This selfish fear to escape and sacrifice his beloved friends to a horrific fate wars with his new-awakened valor. He reasons even Gandalf would agree flight is the only logical choice.

He discards this lie. His friends pledged to protect him. He can do nothing less. But he also reaches for the Ring.

As the battle rages within Frodo, the arm comes closer to Sam. This gives the Ring-bearer the strength to defeat the cowardly temptation to run away. He asserts his will against the Ring and demonstrates to himself it can be done. He grabs a sword and slashes off the hand to save his friends. Frodo also calls upon Tom for help. "Heroism does not necessarily mean standing out from the others as the strongest; it can go hand in hand with reliance upon others. We see that Tolkien is putting forth a new model of the hero, one who does not insist on doing everything himself, but who can accept aid from others" (Gardner et al. 49). Robert Steed echoes this:

> Frodo is often described in secondary literature as a kind of Christ-figure, serving as a type for Christ-as-priest or for Christ-as-suffering-servant. However, Frodo has not fully come into those roles here. Instead, he is the one who, even though the most resistant to the Barrow-wight's spell, still needs aid from outside in order to regain his and his friends' freedom. That is, he is not the liberator, but one of the liberated. (7)

Bombadil comes in answer Frodo's plea, defeats the barrow-wight, and releases the sleeping hobbits from its spell. Tom chooses daggers he found in the barrow for each of them. He accompanies them to the borders of his land and tells them to seek shelter at *The Prancing Pony* at Bree. The Ring-bear hopes all these unexpected delays threw off the pursuit of the Black Riders. At this normally happy and peaceful crossroads of hobbits and men, he learns his hope is vain.

Within the *Pony*, Frodo meets a mysterious man called Strider, who tells him he should quiet Pippin. A subtle movement of grace draws the Ring-bearer's attention to his talkative young cousin who regales the crowded inn with the tale of Bilbo's birthday party. Frodo interrupts the tween before he spills any secrets.

This prevents one disaster, but the Ring causes another. Rather than shunt attention away from it, Frodo attracts it in a most spectacular way. The fell object tries to compel him to put it on, so it can announce itself to some ill will. The hobbit resists, but the Ring is not done with him yet. A patron calls for a song. After a moment of wondering what in the Four Farthings he should sing, Frodo enjoys his time in the spotlight. In the midst of an encore, however, he slips from the table where he danced. To the astonishment of all, he does not only fall but completely disappears. This is all those who are on the watch for anything unusual need to see.

Still invisible, Frodo crawls away until he reaches Strider's table and then removes the Ring. He does not know how the disaster unfolded. He suspects the Ring. The Ranger is the only one who does not seem shocked by these events. He reveals he knows the hobbit's true name and asks for a private audience. Frodo does not quite trust the man's intentions but agrees.

Strider requests permission to accompany the Ring-bearer and his companions. He says Frodo's inexplicable vanishing act has placed them in peril. He tells them how unlikely, nay, impossible, it will be to escape the Black Riders if the hobbits attempt to do so on their own. He says Frodo may "be allowed to go forward" from Bree, but once night comes and the power of their enemies waxes, there will be no hope to elude them (*LotR* I:10, 162). Strider offers to serve as their guard and guide. An earlier draft, when the Ranger was still a hobbit called Trotter, gives some insight into Frodo's thoughts: "He looked at Trotter: grim and wild and rough-clad. . . . he had made Frodo suspect everyone, even Mr. Butterbur. And all his warnings could so well apply to himself. . . . Everything he had said was curiously double-edged. He had a dark look, and yet there was something in his face that was strangely attractive" (*Treason* 46).

Butterbur comes in to give Frodo a letter from Gandalf, which confirms Strider is an ally. The Ring-bearer wonders why the man did not state before he knew the wizard. The Ranger pleads his ignorance of the missive and thought he would have to ask for Frodo's trust before he could prove himself worthy of it. He also notes he wanted to make certain the hobbit was trustworthy himself or was an effort by the Enemy to ensnare him.

Strider makes a faux attempt to claim the Ring to answer Sam's nagging doubts about him. Lucky for them, he is not such a man to harbor such desires. Rather he pledges to save the hobbits from their adversaries, even if it costs him his life to do so.

Frodo shows the first sign of spiritual discernment grace provides him. He sees the noble and humble soul of Aragorn beneath the scruffy appearance of Strider. He notes he reached his judgement of the man's character before Gandalf's letter cemented what his heart already told him. He accepts Strider's offer to accompany them.

Merry rushes in with the alarming news of his encounter with their enemies. Strider protects them during the night while they camp out in the parlor. Frodo wakes suddenly from a deep sleep as evil enters the inn, but he does not know what he senses. He dreams of the assault on Crickhollow and hears the horn of Buckland, but again does not realize his dream reflects an actual happening.

The next morning Strider and the hobbits find the room they would have stayed in searched and vandalized. The Ranger and his companions depart with a pony bought by Barliman to help offset the theft of their other ponies. They begin a zig-zag course to shake off any unfriendly followers the Ranger does not doubt will come.

Battle

The hobbits enjoy their journey with Strider until they spend two miserable days traversing the Midgewater Marshes. They quickly accustom themselves to the rigors of hiking for hours with little to eat. Pippin remarks how much greater a hobbit Frodo is. The Ring-bearer jokes the truth is actually the opposite. He fears he will turn into a ghost if he loses any more weight. Strider quickly puts a stop to the jest. He knows exactly what the hobbit in his ignorance speaks of.

Frodo misses the Shire more than ever. He looks at the "hateful" Road which would take him back home, but which he cannot use (*LotR* I:11, 184). The way of a wanderer Aragorn chose decades ago, but it holds a sharp-edged newness for Frodo. This painful gaze warns him the Black Riders are in close pursuit at last. Strider says the Ring attracts them. Its Bearer greatly fears there is no way to escape them, but the Ranger says not all hope is lost.

Frodo resists an urge to cry out to break the terrible suspense, as they await their enemies at Weathertop. Fear clutches the hobbits in a vise at the approach of the wraiths. Even worse, Frodo feels an overpowering compulsion to put on the Ring. He fights valiantly, but in the end, the coercive force swallows him whole. With the Ring upon his finger, he sees clearly into the wraith-world and beholds the fell and fallen kings as they truly are: terrible remnants of men, whose "keen and merciless eyes . . . fell on him and pierced him" (*LotR* I:11, 191). Frodo draws his sword, but this does not stop the advance of one of his foes.

"At that moment Frodo threw himself forward on the ground, and he heard himself crying aloud: *O Elbereth! Gilthoniel!* At the same time, he struck at the feet of his enemy" (*LotR* I:11, 191). Ralph C. Wood notes:

> Frodo is far more acted upon than acting. . . . Too weak of will to save himself, he is divinely enabled to invoke the star-queen Varda by her elven names. . . . Because Ilúvatar (God) is already present to him, Frodo can still prostrate

himself in the act of prayer. But the prayer itself is miraculously prayed through him . . . much as St. Paul declares in Romans 8:26: 'we do not know how to pray as we ought, but the Spirit himself intercedes for us.' This is an act brought about solely by God. ("Conflict")

Though the Ring-bearer does not physically harm his foe, he delivers a powerful blow in his response to the inspiration to call upon Elbereth. The wraiths withdraw because of this before they can do more than wound his shoulder. With Frodo's last strength, he removes the Ring.

Strider admits his puzzlement over why their enemies fled rather than press their attack. After what Frodo tells him of their assault, he understands. The wound will do their work for him. "It is much more than a mere injury to the flesh, and it is made by no ordinary knife blade. . . . The blade of the Nazgûl is alive inside Frodo, like a kind of cancer" (Gardner, et al. 57-58). The Ranger tells the alarmed hobbits he thinks Frodo will withstand the physical and spiritual attack on his body for a greater length than his foes believe possible.

At dawn, the Ranger discovers the abandoned blade whose point is now at its fell work within Frodo's body. The man crushes *athelas* leaves into hot water and washes the Ring-bearer's shoulder. He admits it may not be strong enough to battle such an evil injury, but it does bring some relief.

Frodo tries to make sense of the violence done to him. He blames himself for the senseless choice to put on the Ring and not to have the strength of will to withstand it. He realizes it was not his decision but obedience to the demand of his enemies. Yet he still holds it against himself he could not withstand the overpowering assault. He has not come far enough in his understanding of fault and compliance to gain the insight the blame is not his. This attack is the first trauma which later amounts to post-traumatic stress. But what could have weakened the Ring-bearer to the point of despair and non-resistance does not. He fights against this enemy now within his own body.

As the shard of the Morgul-blade insidiously inches toward Frodo's heart, he has episodes of disassociation in the form of derealization. The *Diagnostic and Statistical Manual of Mental Disorders (DSM)* defines this: "Persistent or recurrent experiences of unreality of surroundings (e.g. the world around the individual is experienced as unreal, dreamlike, distant, or distorted)" (272). Dark dreams plague the Ring-bearer. The real world grows more shadow-like, and the wraith-world becomes more real. Frodo silently bears his increasing torment, as he and his companions make their way to Rivendell. One night, he suffers a dreadful sense "black shapes were advancing to smother him" (*LotR* I:12, 197). More unsettling is his dream of walking in his own garden, which feels less real to him than the shadowy adversaries he knows stalks him. His wound also begins to affect his vision, as a veil comes between him and the world around him. Other dissociative episodes plague the Ring-bearer during and after the Quest.

The next night, "Frodo lay half in a dream, imagining that endless dark wings were sweeping by above him, and that on the wings rode pursuers that sought him in all the hollows of the hills" (*LotR* I:12, 198-199). This nightmare prefigures the return of the Nazgûl on their fell beasts.

The Ring-bearer's vision continues to worsen as the shard draws him further into the wraith-world. One thing that stalls it a bit is happening upon the same trolls who turned to stone during Bilbo's adventure. Frodo laughs twice, a sound unknown in Mordor. As such, it cannot block the grace such gives the beleaguered hobbit. The hobbit's memory of his uncle's journey and the sunlight that blesses the company strengthens him to resist the evil within him.

After Sam surprises everyone with his song about the troll, Frodo makes a teasing prediction about his gardener's future. Hannah Eagleson remarks:

> It is a good prediction in that it sees that there is more to Sam than meets the eye, and in that it sees that Sam will live a more exciting life than most people expected and will rise admirably to meet its challenges. Some of it does come true: Sam does become something of a warrior in his desire to

protect Frodo, and he certainly has the courage required to wage war in a good cause. (*Wisdom: ROTK* 65-66)

The travelers come to the stone under which the dwarves and Bilbo hid their treasure from the trolls' cave. Frodo vainly desires his uncle brought back naught but that.

For the first time since Weathertop, the hobbits and their guardian hear the fearful noise of pursuit. Frodo's slow transition into the wraith-world allows him to see beyond what mortals normally sense. The bane of the Morgul-knife wound here becomes for a moment a blessing. He sees Glorfindel's true nature as a being of great light. The Elf's grace-filled arrival gives the Ring-bearer a brief reprieve from the physical and spiritual torment of his wound.

Frodo objects after the Elf-lord tells him to ride Asfaloth. He faced and conquered the temptation to desert his friends in the barrow. Now he refuses to do so again. Glorfindel assures him it is right to do so if their enemies come. The hobbit would then not leave his companions in peril but draw it away from them.

By the end of the next day, the Ring-bearer's pain and the veil over his sight worsens. But as the physical world darkens, the veil becomes less pronounced and allows him to feel less isolated.

The next morning, Glorfindel tells of his intuition their enemies are nigh. As the Nazgûl come into view, Frodo slows Asfaloth down. He sees the Riders clearly while the material world around him disappears. The Ring-bearer recognizes his odd reluctance to flee comes from an assault on his will. He brandishes his sword to defy his enemies. Glorfindel's use of the Elven tongue frees the spell-bound horse. Asfaloth leaps toward the Ford of Bruinen with the wraiths in swift pursuit.

The Elven steed flies by one Rider and passes over to the other side. Frodo sees the Nazgûl gathered on the opposite shore and awaits with dread their crossing to seize him and the Ring. He knows there is no escape.

The Ringwraiths again order the Ring-bearer to stop. In what Anna Smol calls "one of Frodo's greatest heroic moments," the hobbit is almost too weak to resist, yet he does (51). The Riders laugh at his defiant demand they cease their pursuit. Though nearly overcome at last, Frodo makes one last stand and boldly invokes the names of Elbereth and Lúthien. The Witch-king demonstrates his terrifying control over the hobbit's body. As the fell wraith draws nigh to Frodo, the River rises to overwhelm him and his comrades.

Near to the threshold of crossing over into the undead world of the Nazgûl, the Ring-bearer sees what appears as white horses amidst the waves. He also glimpses Glorfindel in all his Elven glory. Smol notes:

> Wavering on the boundary between two realms, the Wraith-world and Rivendell, Frodo must exert his greatest powers of will in order to make a choice, but the dangers of surrendering his autonomy to the overpowering forces of Sauron are abundantly clear, and the battle is far from over, since the poisoned knife blade is only one weapon that attempts to accelerate the slower and more insidious work of the Ring itself. (51)

Frodo wakes several days later in Rivendell with Gandalf at his side. The wizard tells him the evil at work within the hobbit almost worsted him. Tom Shippey notes what this would involve:

> . . . a recurrent prospect in *The Lord of the Rings* is for Frodo to be taken by Sauron and tormented till he . . . goes 'under the shadow', worn out by addiction and privation and torture and fear to a state of nothingness like 'the haggard king' of Minas Morgul. This doesn't happen, but no one says it can't. Indeed, Gandalf saw explicitly that it can. (*Road* 148)

Frodo hopes his part in the whole affair of the Ring is over. He considers his long-held desire for adventure satisfied and now longs to return home.

Gandalf praises the Ring-bearer's battle against the shard for over a fortnight. Such a courageous stand even some men could not have made. Frodo expresses relief he did not know what peril he was in or terror would have immobilized him. This echoes the benefits of being ignorant of one's true danger Bilbo had during his adventure. He did not know how close he was to hitting the ceiling as he jumped over Gollum. He also thought he knew what to expect the second time he approached Smaug and so was not afraid. The wizard makes a veiled mention of the aid of Providence in Frodo's valiant struggle.

Gandalf notes a difference in how the hobbit looks and muses about what this means. His guess is a hopeful one: "He may become like a glass filled with a clear light . . ." (*LotR* II:1, 217). Constance G. J. Wagner notes with these

> simple yet evocative words . . . Gandalf is attempting to describe the subtle charisma that Frodo possesses, the Power of Spirit that marks him for the Quest to begin with.
> This 'clear light' can be considered a sign of favour from an unspoken yet ever-present divine Providence - a mark of grace bestowed or even the presence of grace shining through. ("Sacramentum" 83)

Verlyn Flieger observes the implication of Gandalf's musings is "by going deeply into the dark and passing through it, one can come out again into the light on the other side" ("Body" 287).

At the feast to celebrate the victory over the Nazgûl, Frodo beholds Arwen's astonishing beauty.

In the Hall of Fire, the Ring-bearer's fondest desire comes true with a wonderful reunion with Bilbo. Frodo learns his uncle was Sam's constant companion in anxious vigil while Elrond struggled to heal him. Bilbo says he sometimes considered returning home to retrieve the Ring, but Gandalf and Elrond were against this. Now with it before him once more, it becomes fearfully clear his lust for it was not cured but dormant. He cannot resist asking to see it. Frodo hesitates but complies. He jerks his hand back, as his uncle appears in a vision to change into a Gollum-like creature he has to actively choose not to hit. "The insidious power of the Ring to infect healthy relationships with greed and selfishness comes to affect one of the happiest bonds in the novel - the friendship between Bilbo and Frodo" (Gardner et al. 58). That the ancient hobbit names the younger not only his physical heir but also passes along the role of storyteller and scribe is "something sacred about Bilbo and Frodo's relationship that makes it all the more painful to see the Ring come between them" (Gardner et al. 58).

Frodo's horrified reaction to his uncle's transformation helps him realize more than ever the Ring's corrupting and malignant nature, as well as how possessive of it he is himself. It puts into sharp relief the future he and Bilbo will have if they give themselves totally to their Ring-lust. But not even this frighteningly enlightening experience can long come between them. Bilbo's awareness of the dreadful hold the Ring holds over its bearers prompts him to profusely apologize.

Andrew Seeley speaks of the time the Ring-bearer and Sam spend in the Hall:

> Sam and Frodo recognize what a privilege it is to hear the Elves tell their great stories of triumph and sorrow, of beauty and betrayal. More than that, they experience the stories as they were meant to be told - chanted and sung in the Hall of Fire by the greatest story-tellers. . . . Here story-telling is not a segregated activity - the rhythms of the life of Rivendell are governed by their passion for stories and songs. This is what drew Bilbo to come back when he left the Shire. He was also a story-teller. The atmosphere of the place led him to dare (with a daring only a hobbit would have) to express undying beauties in clumsy mortal words, enough to fill the three volumes that he will later pass on to Frodo. ("Education")

Frodo has a profound experience as a mortal within an Elven realm: ". . . visions of far lands and bright things that he had never yet imagined opened out before him; and the firelit hall became like a golden mist above seas of foam that sighed upon the margins of the world" (LotR II:1, 227).

After the Ring-bearer begins to dream, the waking world intrudes and combines with it. Bilbo's recitation of his poem about Eärendil becomes the bridge between them. Stephen C. Winter comments, "Frodo has for a moment been given an insight into the nature of the story of which he is now a part" ("Sam asks"). He hears the Great Music. This gives the first hint of how his and Eärendil's story intertwine. Both sacrifice all to save Middle-earth: Frodo goes East, Eärendil goes West. The man cannot return to his home after he reaches the Undying Lands. Frodo finds no place to be at rest in Middle-earth after the ordeal to reach Mordor. Judith Klinger notes how deeply this time affects Frodo: "Elvish music and poetry . . . open up a new space of imagination that Frodo enters . . . , even if the images and impressions remain unreadable to him. Rather, the fluid interweaving of vision, enchantment and dream illustrates that Frodo is slipping back and forth across the boundaries between different kinds of perception" ("Strange Powers" 77). Cami Agan agrees:

> Frodo seems to intuit the holiness of the space and sound within the Hall of Fire. . . . As listener, Frodo crosses through the portal between consciousness and dream by means of Elven song, and as such the narrative again creates a unique relationship between the Ringbearer and the Elven Stories.
>
> . . .
>
> . . . Frodo's repeated visions and dreams suggest that he attains special knowledge and foresight through songs or references to the ancient Story and, perhaps, that he is able to be drawn further than other mortals into Faërie through these moments.
>
> . . .
>
> . . . As Frodo and Bilbo leave the Hall, . . . Frodo is drawn back into the enchantment of the Elven voices in prayer. Literally in the passageway between the divine rejoicing and the 'homely' talk they seek together, the hobbits embody the position of the worshipper still involved in the world of the 'now' yet continually drawn to the world of the sacred, the mortal who finds joy in the immortal. Frodo in particular yearns for the enchantment or 'dream time' of the prayer to Elbereth. . . . At the same time,

he remains connected to Middle-earth, to his hobbit nature, and to Bilbo. . . . (54, 57, 58)

The next morning, Elrond introduces Frodo to the others gathered at the Council to determine the fate of the Ring. The Elf-lord notes its members may seem made up by chance of all the Free Peoples who just happened to come at the same time on different errands. But he is clear chance has nothing to do it. They and only they were gathered from distant lands and different cultures on purpose for this one purpose.

All listen as Elrond begins the long tale of the history of the Ring. Wonder fills Frodo to hear the Elf-lord was present with Gil-galad at Sauron's defeat thousands of years before. Marvel comes again to hear of the lineage of Aragorn. The hobbit thinks the man should have the Ring. The Ranger denies this and confirms Frodo as its proper custodian.

Gandalf asks Frodo to show everyone the Ring. The hobbit "was shaken by a sudden shame and fear; and he felt a great reluctance to reveal the Ring, and a loathing of its touch" (*LotR* II:2, 240).

The time comes for Bilbo to give his part of the story. He looks at Glóin and asks for forgiveness if this version is different from the one he originally gave.

Gandalf mentions the providential timing of Sauron's flight from Dol Guldur and how this is tied to Bilbo passing through Mirkwood.

The Council discusses and discards several options to dispose of the Ring. "Frodo . . . felt a dead darkness in his heart" (*LotR* II:2, 260).

Elrond dismisses Boromir's argument against the Ring's destruction. The only viable option to pursue is such destruction and the Road into the heart of their Enemy's realm. Bilbo volunteers to take up the task. He thinks the Elf-lord considers him responsible for the mess and so responsible to clean it up. He does not like the time it will take away from his book. He is nonetheless willing to do it. But Bilbo was created for another purpose. This he performed perfectly: to be Ring-finder and to shelter its future Bearer.

Gandalf politely refuses the ancient hobbit. This gladdens Bilbo, but he wonders who will go in his place. Frodo looks around at the other Council members, but no one puts forth a name. "A great dread fell on him, as if he was waiting the pronouncement of some doom that he had long foreseen and vainly hoped might after all never be spoken" (*LotR* II:2, 263). Edmund Fuller notes, ". . . both Gandalf and Frodo, each in his way, appear not as Christ equivalents, but as partial anticipations of the Christ. With Frodo, quite simply and movingly, it lies in his vain wish that the cup might be taken from him, and since it may not, he goes his long, dolorous way as Ring-bearer - a type of the Cross-bearer to come" (35).

After a long struggle, Frodo resists his great desire to remain with Bilbo. To his own astonishment, he gives aloud his answer to the call he heard in the silence of his heart and soul. He chooses to forsake his own safety and desires and embrace instead insecurity and the desire of Another. He wills to carry upon his shoulders, around his neck, and within his heart, mind, and soul the crushing weight of Sauron's terrible darkness and hatred. Fear, doubt, hunger, thirst, torment: it all lies ahead. But as great as Sauron's malice proves, the awe-some love the Ring-bearer holds for Middle-earth and Ilúvatar and the Powers hold for him is far greater. Though Gerald May does not speak of Frodo, his words still apply: ". . . the power of grace flows most fully when human will chooses to act in harmony with divine will" (139). Trudy G. Shaw and A. K. Frailey observe:

> One of my favorite religious works of art is a painting that shows the calling of the prophet Samuel as a boy. The picture shows him listening intently to God's message, but this didn't happen until after he'd misunderstood the call three times, thinking it had come from Eli. At that point, the Bible tells us, Samuel "did not yet know the LORD," but, as Eli instructs him, the next time Samuel is called he responds with a statement that leaves him open to whatever God might ask: "Speak, for your servant is listening." It seems to me that Frodo at the Council is in a situation similar to Samuel's. Like Samuel, he has already left his home but

doesn't know what his next step will be. He does "not yet know the LORD," but responds to the call as far as he understands it. (Shaw, "I will take")

Frodo was not given an order, but he knew all too well that he had a call which only he could answer. He knew, deep into the recesses of his being, that there was no escaping the trials which awaited him. His best hope lay in his obedience to the fate which was at his feet. He could have refused the burden set before him. It was not only his love for others that put strength into his fearful will but also the sure knowledge that something much greater than anything he could imagine was at work, and it was best not to refuse to do one's part. Even though he could not see himself succeeding, he thought it better to die in the effort than to refuse the challenge that awaited him. Life or death was not the overriding issue. Doing that which he was called to do was the focus. (Frailey 60)

Thomas Finch notes, "Long ago, Abraham made a journey of faith when God said to him, 'Leave your country, your people and your father's household and go to the land I will show you' (Genesis 12:1). He hadn't asked to be uprooted and go into an unfamiliar territory, but Abraham 'obeyed and went, even though he did not know where he was going' (Hebrews 11:8) (111-112)." Jentezen Franklin also speaks of this divine call: Abraham had "[t]he ability to hear God . . . to believe what God said . . . to denounce security for the sake of God's mission . . . to stay focused on the mission . . . to accomplish the mission" (186). Virtually word for word, this is Frodo's experience as well.

After the hobbit's astounding words, Elrond gazes upon the newly confirmed Ring-bearer. "Frodo felt his heart pierced by the sudden keenness of the glance" (LotR II:2, 264). The Elf-lord already noted power and sound knowledge alone would not give anyone the ability to travel for long on the dreadful Road now before Frodo. At Bag End, Gandalf said the hobbit was not chosen for these qualities. Indeed, Ilúvatar chose him because he did not have them. His powerlessness and his humility to rely on others for aid make him an ideal Ring-bearer. If pride, ambition, or native power deluded him with the conviction he knew all the answers and need not trust anything but his own counsel, the Ring could corrupt him far easier. But empty of a need to control things, Frodo becomes a malleable instrument for Providence to use. If he used his own power solely, he would have failed, but never does he operate so.

The Ring-bearer offers the sacrifice and is the sacrifice. He embraced this destiny at Bag End for the short term. Now he does for the long term. And after a personal knowledge of the peril to his body, mind, and soul from the evil which pursues him, almost devoured him, and which he now carries against his heart. ". . . Frodo's temperament suits him to the great task before him. . . . Resisting the temptation of the Ring is a matter of conviction and inner strength. Elrond's description of the ideal Ring-bearer - who is . . . morally steady [and] willing to sacrifice himself for the good of humanity - constitutes a fair description of a Christian saint" (Gardner et al. 62). Frodo lives St. Paul's words long before the man writes them: "For it is when I am weak that I am strong" (2 Cor. 12:10).

Elrond understands Ilúvatar's will woven throughout the tale of the Ring now includes this. Indeed, Frodo's fearful and courageous embrace of his calling so impresses the Elf-lord, he names him among the greatest heroes of all the Children of Ilúvatar throughout the ages.

Bilbo tells Frodo they will enjoy a good amount of time together. They can work on his book and begin the one which concerns the upcoming Quest. The elder Baggins remains set on a happy ending to both. The younger agrees such would be good, but he doubts reality will match his uncle's desire.

Yet even Frodo cannot hold long onto his worries in Elrond's fair house. All of the hobbits fully enjoy their extended stay without any trouble over what their future holds, just as Bilbo and the dwarves had their spirits restored decades before.

As the year fails, Elrond asks Frodo to confirm his decision made at the Council. After he does so, the Elf-lord appoints the rest of the companions who will walk with him and Sam. Gandalf and Pippin have to talk him into allowing the tween and Merry based on their love and loyalty to Frodo.

Bilbo bequeaths the priceless gifts of Sting and the *mithril* shirt. Frodo has the same reaction his uncle did to the latter. These protect his body, while love protects his heart and soul.

> Sting . . . provides a link between Frodo, Bilbo, and the much larger, multi-Age wars between good and evil in Middle-earth. . . . Sting represents . . . the heroic greatness of those battles, in which good Elves fought orcs many years before Frodo came onto the scene. While Frodo may be a small Hobbit in the middle of grand doings in the world, he is as vital a part of that struggle against Evil as any ancient Elven hero. (Shmoop Editorial Team, "Sting")

Frodo tries to thank Bilbo for all the gifts given down their years together. The ancient hobbit only wishes for his beloved heir not to take any unnecessary risks and to look out for anything to include in his book. His simple action of picking up a ring in the dark with little thought stirred to life what will now transpire. As difficult as it is to know Frodo must travel down an arduous, hopeless Road because of this, how much worse for the fate of the world if he did not. Bilbo recites a poem that speaks of what has come before and what will come after he passes from this life. It includes his longing already to hear the beloved son of his heart return safe and sound.

But the Ring-bearer's journey has no promise of this.

Tests

"The process in Celtic Christianity was that of a quest, becoming a *peregrini* or pilgrim. It included the willingness to become a stranger and to leave behind one's own comforts, possessions, certainties and systems of control . . ." (Dearborn 139).

Before dark, Elrond and his household, including Bilbo, bid farewell to the Company. Each continues his journey as a *peregrini*, just as the ancient hobbit himself did decades before.

The Company travels for a fortnight before they reach Hollin. The sun shows its face for the first time and gladdens Frodo's heart. But even in this once safe land there is danger. After Sam and Aragorn see the *crebain*, the Ranger realizes spies are already on the look out. Frodo senses more than birds seek them.

Three days later, the Company reaches Caradhras. Frodo overhears Aragorn and Gandalf speak of their Road. The Ranger favors continuing above ground toward the Redhorn Gate. The wizard advocates another path, which Aragorn firmly opposes. Frodo is glad the man's choice prevails, but soon the mountain torments them with malicious glee. Boromir rescues the Ring-bearer from hypothermia.

Near dawn snow ends its assault. After the Company climbs down the mountain, they debate their next steps. A return to Rivendell is out of the question, no matter how inviting it seems. Gandalf notes they could not attempt another journey with any hope of stealth. The Ring would stay there until reclaimed and the Elven haven laid waste. Such a bleak forecast convinces Frodo the only chance for success lays forward but which way?

Gandalf proposes the dark underground path through Moria. Boromir puts forth two alternate routes, but the wizard discounts them as too dangerous. The sound of howling wolves decides the matter for them.

After many miles, the Company reaches the Door into Moria. Fear reaches out to Frodo. He does not know its source until the Watcher in the Water snatches him. It does not pass beneath Gandalf's notice the beast specifically targets the Ring-bearer. Frodo demonstrates the astonishing ability hobbits have to quickly recover from traumatic events by how easily he puts this terrifying encounter behind him.

The Company travels without mishap for several days through this once great dwarven kingdom, now a stronghold of their enemies. Frodo has better night vision because of his Morgul-wound. Its lingering effects also make him more aware of the oppressive evil around him. He remains silent about all he senses, which includes mysterious sounds like footsteps behind them.

Amazement fills Frodo to learn from Gandalf the true value of the coat of mail he secretly wears. The hobbit mightily desires to return to the carefree days he shared with Bilbo when he did not know of the dangers outside their land.

While on watch, Frodo sees from a distance what looks like eyes. He convinces himself he dreamed it. Dream or not, the eyes advance toward him.

After orcs come upon them with a cave-troll, Frodo uses the rage that flares up in him to strike at the troll's foot. At the end of a fierce battle, a mighty orc throws his spear at the Ring-bearer. Aragorn dispatches the foe and picks up what he assumes is the hobbit's corpse. But then the corpse speaks.

The Company makes their way out of the chamber and down the stairs. As they await Gandalf, Sam holds Frodo in his arms. The wizard expresses his great delight to hear the Ring-bearer's voice.

Ilúvatar's protective guard over the Company shows itself once more as they come near to the Bridge of Khazad-dûm. If the orcs had not launched their attack when and where they did, the Walkers would have taken another path and become trapped on the same side of a great fire as their enemies. But the orcs did attack. It altered the Walkers' route, and now the fire separates them.

An orc arrow strikes Frodo, but his *mithril* coat stops it. At the Bridge, Gandalf engages their most fearsome enemy. To the great shock of the Company, the Balrog's whip entangles the wizard's legs and drags him down with it.

The Walkers flee the darkness of one Black Pit to fall into another. Aragorn's foresight of the terrible peril which awaited

Gandalf personally shakes each to their core. But it does not alter their commitment to their mission.

As the Company travels on, the Ring-bearer again hears footsteps and sees eyes behind them, or at least he thinks he does.

As the Walkers cross the stream Nimrodel, Frodo senses a musical voice within the waters. They sleep that night in the trees with Haldir and his brothers.

Hours later, Frodo wakes and senses peril close by. Something starts to climb and gets close enough for him to see eyes. There is no doubt this time whether this is real or imagined. Haldir reports he saw the creature too before it fled back into the woods. He says he did not shoot at it because he did not want to alert the orcs who pursue the Company. All unknowingly, he saves the Quest from disaster.

Deep into Lórien, the Elves blindfold the Walkers. Frodo's other senses heighten to give him a profound experience: ". . . it seemed to him that he had stepped over a bridge of time into a corner of the Elder Days, and was now walking in a world that was no more" (*LotR* II:6, 340).

Not until the next afternoon does the Company see again. Frodo's physical eyes marvel at what his heart has already feasted on. This wondrous Elven realm is both vividly new and old beyond telling. Ralph C. Wood notes, "It's almost as if he were Adam, the first person to behold the newly minted world . . ." (*Gospel* 20). Even though evil stalks its borders, it remains inviolate. Frodo's Quest dooms his body to leave, but a spiritual part of him walks amongst the trees long after. He hears water from a great distance beat upon beaches that were no more and the cries of extinct birds. He touches the bark of a tree and feels how joyously alive it is. These incredibly intense sensations give him a foretaste of his life in the West.

Frodo sees Caras Galadhon in the distance and feels a tremendous longing to get there faster than his feet can carry him. The hobbit exists in both the Elven and the drab mortal world. The former draws him more and more, just as it does Bilbo. The Ring-bearer sees a vision of the time Aragorn and Arwen plighted their troth here decades previously. Neither hobbit nor man return in their mortal forms to this place again.

Haldir leads the Company to the Lord and Lady of the Wood. Galadriel reveals they know the perilous task of the Walkers and how easily it could fail. But this is not a foregone conclusion provided they all remain dedicated to their mission. After she tests each of their hearts, all but Frodo remark on the experience.

The Company hear the Elves lament the loss of Gandalf. Frodo makes his own song to commemorate the wizard, though in the past he rarely touched upon this particular method of sub-creation.

After some time, the Ring-bearer becomes aware his sojourn in this blessed land is almost over. Sam wishes to see Elven magic, but Frodo does not. His mystical experiences of the Elven realms of Rivendell and Lórien already drown his senses in deep wonder.

The hobbits see Galadriel walk toward them. After she brings them to her Mirror, she asks Frodo if he wishes to look inside. She leaves the decision entirely up to him, but she does think he has the ability to bear what he may see.

Unlike Sam, Frodo sees nothing of the Shire, but scenes from thousands of years in the past to the future ship he will take to the Undying Lands. He sees the resurrected Gandalf, though he is not certain who he sees. He beholds the Sea for the first time, as well as the coming battle of Minas Tirith he will never witness but here. The only scene he truly recognizes is the welcome sight of Bilbo, not in the Shire, but in Rivendell. This gives another sign such rarefied realms fill the hearts and souls of both Bagginses more than their homeland can.

After Frodo thinks he sees all the Mirror has to show him, the Eye of Sauron appears and terrifies him. This experience teaches him a vital lesson: though he plainly sees his Enemy, his Enemy cannot see him. The Dark Lord actively seeks to do so, but the hobbit realizes he will remain hidden unless he makes the conscious decision to reveal himself. After the Ring tries to coerce this choice, Galadriel's voice stops it.

The light of Eärendil's Star shines upon the Lady. Frodo marvels to discern one of the Three Elven Rings upon her finger.

Galadriel tells the hobbit of the terrible doom that hangs over the Elves of Middle-earth because the Ring exists. If Frodo fails in his Quest and Sauron reclaims the Ring, all will fall under the Dark Lord's terrible dominion, including the Elven strongholds that have long held out against him. If Frodo succeeds, the realms of the Elves will still fall into ruin. They will not succumb to the Shadow but to the relentless march of time. Weighed down by this, the Ring-bearer asks Galadriel what she would desire to happen. She absolves him of any guilt or responsibility he may feel for this doom. He must do what he must do. She tells of two vain wishes: either Sauron never forged the Ring or it was never found again after its loss millennia ago. But as both did happen, she accepts the fate of the Elves as given. All that happens and will happen is in the hands of Ilúvatar. There she is content to leave it. It is beyond her control, and so she does not trouble herself further.

Frodo makes one last attempt to disentangle himself from his own doom as Ring-bearer.
Galadriel gives a hint of what the hobbit's trial was during her silent interrogation of the Company. She acknowledges the sharpness of Frodo's spiritual insights into hearts. She confesses to fantasies about what she would do if she claimed the Ring as her own. With the hobbit's offer, he places her on the threshold of their fulfillment.

As Galadriel battles on the knife-edge of claiming or denying the Ring's immense power, Frodo beholds in a vision what she would be if she grasped it. The Lady emerges victorious from the struggle and solidifies the hobbit's determination to fully embrace at last the terrible doom fallen upon him. He did so in bits and pieces before, but up to this point, still wished to avoid it if he could. Galadriel's transformation shows him this is no longer an option. This task is his and only his. He is the conduit through which she receives grace and victory over her own Ring-lust; she is the instrument through which he obtains the strength to bear his burden.

> Frodo and Gimli . . . make immense progress in becoming reconciled to that which is other in their lives. Frodo becomes reconciled to his own very cruciform vocation. He is more than willing not only to reveal to Galadriel the ring he is carrying, but also to relinquish it to her. She reveals that

it is his cup to drink, his vocation to carry the ring, and to give it up where it can be finally and fully destroyed. Through the refreshment and gifting of the Elves, Frodo is more fully empowered to endure the immense burden of the ring, to see the implication of his fulfillment of this calling or of his failure. (Dearborn 145)

Celeborn and Galadriel hold a farewell feast for the Company. Frodo concentrates his attention on the Lady rather than the food. Though he remains in body a hobbit, his perceptions here are more Elven. Again he sees the dual nature of time within such lands.

The Company receives many gifts before and after the feast. For the Quest proper, the most important are the life- and soul-sustaining *lembas* beard, the phial filled with water reflecting the light of a Silmaril, and rope. After Frodo receives the star-glass, he has another mystical experience, as he sees Galadriel through it. Nicole Topham notes, "By giving Frodo the phial, Galadriel reminds Frodo that even though he is neither an elf nor a man, he is akin to the heroes of the past, a spiritual descendent, if you will, carrying on simply another leg in the long quest to preserve Middle-earth. He is another Eärendil" (I:329).

As the Company departs, Galadriel sings. Frodo does not comprehend the words, but they burn into his memory. He translates it later and realizes it ends with a prayer he may find the way West.

The Walkers become riders as they travel for days upon the River Anduin. One night, Gollum reappears, but the Ring-bearer frightens him off. Several nights later, orcs attack near the rapids of Sarn Gebir. An arrow strikes Frodo, but his dwarf-mail protects him. Legolas shoots down a flying beast. The Ring-bearer suspects a Nazgûl is near based on how his body reacts akin to after the Morgul-knife wounded him.

Fear in the form of reverential awe comes over Frodo at the sight of the Argonath. He sees as in a vision the King who guides his boat at the moment a long-held desire reaches fulfillment. Frodo and Sam are afraid, but Aragorn is home.

The Company reaches Parth Galen a week and a half after they leave the Golden Wood. The next morning, Aragorn announces they must decide the Road they will take, either as a group or individually. Fear still holds the Ring-bearer bound. To go to Mordor, where he knows he must, means naught but suffering and death. To rest first in Minas Tirith would only delay the inevitable and would likely prove disastrous. Frodo asks for time alone before he makes his decision. None but Boromir watch where the hobbit goes off to wrestle with his duty and anxiety.

Though Frodo wanders physically by himself, he is not truly alone. Memories of his homeland and of Gandalf's words surround him. After a while, the hobbit senses an enemy invade the search of his heart and soul. He looks behind him and sees only Boromir. Yet his sense of a nearby adversary is not wrong.

The warrior tries to convince Frodo to come with him to Gondor. The man wants to accomplish what seems to make sense in the short term: use the Ring to triumph over Sauron. The hobbit's willingness to embrace the wisdom of others, as well as his awareness a spiritual war must be waged alongside the physical one, allows him to see the long-term effects of such a 'victory.' He knows he must not delay his doom.

Boromir does not recognize the peril of the Ring as Frodo and others of the Wise do. He continues to press for the Ring-bearer to come to Minas Tirith and gives several reasons why this is the wisest choice. The hobbit will have none of it. After the man cannot convince Frodo with words, he tries to use his superior physical strength to wrest the Ring from him. Its Bearer watches the man's fair face horrifically transform, as lust for the Ring burns within, just as Bilbo's did in Rivendell. Frodo has no choice but to put the Ring on to escape his erstwhile ally.

The Ring-bearer comes upon Amon Hen. His vision ranges over a wide area: all scenes of war. Hope flares at the sight of Minas Tirith; it dies as he looks upon the Enemy's Dark Tower. Here he senses the Eye perceive him. He listens to himself announce two contrary things: defiant refusal of his adversary and a willingness to come to him. Frodo does not know which is true. Amidst this confusion, two overwhelming powers vie to dominate him. Pinned down in agony by the terrible pressure to either claim the Ring or to remove it, he reaches a moment where neither force reaches him, where he is only himself. He recognizes his freedom to make his own choice. In this instant, he decides to remove the Ring. If he delayed just a moment longer, Sauron would have pinpointed him. Instead, the Eye passes him by. Frodo learns again from the great lesson begun in the barrow: even while under assault from the terrifying power of evil, he can still choose to resist it using his own strength of will.

> . . . Amon Hen serves as a dramatic representation of the role of free will and the part it plays in the battle between reason and desire. Frodo, in saying that he is affected by duty and desire, but not totally identified with either, describes the condition of every human being. . . . What makes Frodo unique is that he is willing to meditate on the matter. His introspective moment at Amon Hen is a time of self-exploration, which in turn is a sign of wisdom. . . . Frodo's wisdom also distinguishes himself from characters like Boromir, for example, who are inordinately subject to stormy fits of passion and desire. (Gardner et al. 80-81)

In the aftermath of this painful but illuminating struggle, and in light of the fear and anguish of Boromir's fall, the Ring-bearer embraces his doom ever more tightly. He makes the brave but foolish decision to go off on his own before the Ring can corrupt anyone else. Patricia Meyer Spacks, Tom Hillman, and Jane Chance note how profoundly this experience shapes Frodo:

> Frodo himself comes to realize that he must not refuse the burden that is laid on him; this realization is his weapon against the temptations of Boromir. . . . This is also what sustains him in his dreadful journey across the Land of Mordor toward the Crack of Doom, and what sustains his hobbit companion, Sam, when he thinks Frodo is killed and knows he must go on. The responsibility involved here, and

throughout the epic, is not simply to one's individual integrity; it is cosmic responsibility, justified by the existence of some vast, unnamed power for good. (Spacks 89)

The gentle phrases 'the Ring must leave them' and 'now Boromir has fallen into evil' reveal the pity that Frodo feels for the man of Gondor, quite unlike the purely harsh words he had had for Gollum, when he rejected out of hand Gandalf's suggestion that pity was in order. . . . Then, too, he had scorned the idea that seeing Gollum would move him to pity, but here seeing does precisely that, not only for Boromir, but potentially for others, too. (Hillman, "Boromir")

A battle is staged within his psyche, and he is pulled first one way, then another, until, as a fully developed moral hero, he exercises the faculty of free will with complete self- control. . . . He feels the struggle of the 'two powers' within him. . . . In this incident, parallel to the encounter of the Riders at the Ford . . . , Frodo here rescues *himself* instead of being rescued by Glorfindel or Gandalf. Further, in proving his moral education by the realization that he must wage his own quest alone to protect both their mission and the other members of the Fellowship, he displays *fortitudo et sapientia* (fortitude and wisdom) and *caritas* (charity) - hence, he acts as that savior of the Fellowship earlier witnessed in the figures of Tom Bombadil and Strider . . . and Gandalf and Galadriel. . . . His education complete, Frodo can now function as a hero for he understands he may, at any time, become a 'monster.' (Chance 161; emphasis in original)

Frodo puts the Ring back on, which oddly and fortunately Sauron does not detect. "Tolkien clearly shows Frodo . . . voluntarily . . . committing himself to the fate . . . appointed for him. His free will accepts his fate. Other examples are easily passed over in the flow of the narrative but stand out clearly when words like *fate, choice, must*, and *will* are highlighted (Flieger, "Music" 34; emphasis in original).

Sauron almost had his victory here but assurance of defeat is the only option for him now. "Frodo thus transforms his whisper of compliance to Sauron into the means of his [Sauron's] destruction: Frodo will come to Sauron but as an infiltrator, not a slave" (Chism 86).

While the Company awaits the hobbit's return, they debate what his path should be. Aragorn says none of them should try to influence or force their own desires for the Ring-bearer on him. Even if they made the attempt, they would find no success. The man knows Frodo's fate is not theirs to design or bend to their own will. "There are other powers at work far stronger" (*LotR* II:10, 394).

Boromir returns to the Company and tells of Frodo's disappearance. Sam discerns something spooked his master so greatly, it served as the necessary catalyst for him to decide what path to take. Richard Mathews notes, "As Frodo and Sam set off on the last stage of the quest together, they are linked by an image of lightning - a flash of sudden insight through empathy - by their past companionship, and by a bond of love and dedication . . . which makes clear a fellowship far deeper than any we have yet seen" (31). Sam races to where the Company left the boats and marvels to see one of them leave the shore with no one on board. He nearly drowns before Frodo rescues him. The elder hobbit takes off the Ring and upbraids Sam for being such a bother. He would already be gone if Sam had not delayed him.

Astonishment fills the humble gardener for Frodo to think he would be all right without him. Sam states he will die if he does not accompany his master; his master tells him the opposite is true. The gardener stubbornly stands his ground. His loyalty and devotion touches Frodo's heart, and the grace of laughter releases him from the stress of the day. Sam gives this gift more than once to ease the Ring-bearer's nearly unremitting torment. Frodo's irritation at delay dissolves into happiness his friend will remain with him. He realizes his and Sam's fates intertwine.

Sauron arrays seemingly invincible power against those who oppose him. His enemies, however, carry a weapon mightier than any of his, one which the Dark Lord has no defense against and cannot prepare for: love. "And Sam's friendship is the only thing that lightens Frodo's natural disposition towards melancholy and sorrow. After being caught up in dark thoughts about war, Sam's honest attachment to him gives Frodo a 'sudden warmth and gladness.' So Sam's friendship for Frodo is their best weapon against the slow, creeping despair that the Ring brings to him" (Shmoop Editorial Team, "Friendship").

As Frodo and Sam travel through the Emyn Muil, they are uncertain of their path. With beautiful child-like faith, the Ring-bearer trusts a way will open. All he needs to do is to continue in obedience. His faith is perhaps even stronger than those in later ages who come to know God and still have trouble in this area. He does not know though whether a force allied with him or set against him will reveal the proper route. Gerald May speaks of the dark night of the soul, but his words apply as well to the Ring-bearer: "But if we *know we don't know* what's happening, we are much more likely to let God lead us. Then, John says, we do not stumble. We are kept safe" (224; emphasis in original). Also applicable is Thomas Finch's observation: "The courageous nature of faith is revealed through steps made in the dark. First steps may be a bit tentative, but they must be taken. Each step will grow stronger" (131). Now is the time Frodo "comes into his own as a worthy adversary for Sauron" (Wagner, "War" I:339).

The next morning, the hobbits speak of Gollum, who they saw two nights previously. Frodo considers the Shadow in the far distance a much greater threat. He feels terribly exposed to the Eye he senses there. As they travel on, they hear or imagine signs Gollum has not given up his pursuit. Or is it the wind?

As a storm approaches, Frodo and Sam attempt to find a way out from the Emyn Muil. The gardener wants to wait until they can see better, but the Ring-bearer sets his will firmly against this. Amidst thunder and lightning, he begins his descent down the cliff. They hear the same shrill yell that frightened them in the Shire. As unnerving as it was then, it is far worse now. The Ring-bearer loses his grip and slides down a short distance. He finds himself without sight. He does not know whether a completely black night fell around him or he has truly gone blind. But there is perhaps another reason. He later experiences a similar vision loss at Minas Morgul, again with Nazgûl near.

As a hard rain starts, Sam says he will come down to his master. Frodo replies there is no point without rope. As the gardener lowers it down, the Ring-bearer's vision begins to return. He realizes this is not a coincidence. In this blessed Elven gift, he recognizes luck has again graced them. Once back on top of the cliff, Frodo thinks the rope is long enough for them to use it to get to the bottom. Sam again counsels his master to wait. He rightly guesses the nature of the terrifying yell they heard and does not think they should go anywhere until morning. The Ring-bearer wants to press on without further delay. He hates the sensation of watchfulness he perceives from Mordor.

Frodo is not quite as confident of the rope as Sam is, but he finds he must place his faith in it. With its blessed aid, they reach the bottom. The gardener is not at all happy to leave the rope behind. After he reconciles himself to its loss, he touches it a final time. Amazement fills the hobbits to see it fall down to them. In another breakthrough of grace, Frodo laughs and teases Sam for not tying the knot tight enough. His guardian defends himself and the knot. He cannot convince his master otherwise, but he believes this is another manifestation of Elven magic.

The hobbits walk a little further before Frodo is tired enough to agree to stop. In the next breath, though, he says he would continue on until he dropped from exhaustion, if the exact route of the Road ahead was more apparent.

After a while, Frodo tells Sam he will take guard duty while Sam sleeps. But before the gardener settles down, they spy Gollum, as he crawls down a cliff. After the creature slips, Sam tries to capture him. But the hobbit is no match for Gollum's strength. Only after Frodo threatens him with Sting does the wicked being release his prisoner.

Sam wants to take the necessary steps to make sure Gollum is no longer a threat. There is no desire in Frodo's heart to let their pursuer die, slowly or quickly. The creature has not hurt them. Sam disagrees, for he felt Gollum's sharp teeth and bets the miserable wretch intends more harm. Frodo agrees this is likely true, but he refuses to punish their spy for a crime not yet committed. He hears his own voice calling for Gollum's death back in Bag End and Gandalf's words against it. His memory does not recall it exactly but adapts it for his present circumstance. He inserts into the wizard's words something Gandalf never actually said. "Then be not too eager to deal out death in *the name of justice, fearing for your own safety*" (*LotR* IV:1, 601; emphasis added).

> The wisdom of Gandalf would be a critical source of guidance for Frodo throughout his life. From an unsettling first conversation shortly after Bilbo's disappearance to life-and-death choices made while confronting the forces of darkness, Frodo gleaned great insight whenever he listened to his friend, mentor, and counselor - insight he would have missed had he allowed the arrogance of youth or the self-satisfaction of pride to get in the way of that vital skill of the wise: the willingness to learn from those wiser still. (Bruner and Ware 21)

Anne Petty remarks, ". . . Gollum represents what Frodo could become if his humanity - his basic goodness and unselfishness - disappears into the Ring's enveloping evil" (217). Had Frodo murdered his adversary, he would have indeed vanished. Instead the Ring provides a good it does not intend and which is critical to its destruction. Under its unwitting tutelage, its Bearer now knows the meaning of suffering. Thomas Finch's words are again applicable: "Suffering has a way of humbling us and changing our views of people and relationships. We realize our oneness with all of suffering humanity. . . . And if we never suffer, we have little comfort to offer to others" (101).

Frodo speaks aloud to Gandalf to assure him pity has entered his heart, and Gollum is safe with him. Ilúvatar grants him this same pity and mercy at the end of the Quest because he grants it first to a fellow creature, a child of Eru like himself. Tolkien noted, "To 'pity' [Gollum], to forbear to kill him, was piece of folly, or a mystical belief in the ultimate value-in-itself of pity and generosity even if disastrous in the world of time" (*Letters* 234).

Frodo is quite aware of Gollum is up to no good. He judges their potential adversary, however, on the basis of concrete, present reality rather than nebulous, future possibility. Just because Gollum *might* harm them is not enough for the Ring-bearer to condemn him. He refuses to give into his fear and makes the same conscious decision to withdraw his hand from striking the creature down as Bilbo did. Ilúvatar allows Gollum's path to cross with Frodo's, so they both learn the wretched creature is not past redemption. Frodo earnestly works to reach the suffering hobbit trapped within the horrid being and to desire Sméagol's cure. He starts by calling him by his given name. So begins his "gradual education to the nobility of service to the unlovable and of perception of damaged good in the corrupt" (Tolkien, *Letters* 329).

Frodo tells Gollum he must come with them and aid them if possible. The creature asks why the hobbits are in such desolate lands. The Ring-bearer bluntly tells them their destination and guesses rightly the Road to Mordor is not unknown to their spy.

As the hobbits listen, Gollum recalls his torment in the Dark Country. An interesting bit of dialogue between the Ring-bearers highlights Frodo's concern and spiritual discernment of Sméagol's soul:

> "'Don't ask Sméagol. Poor, poor Sméagol, he went away long ago. They took his Precious, and he's lost now.'
>
> 'Perhaps we'll find him again, if you come with us,' said Frodo." (*LotR* IV:2, 602)

Gollum still wishes to refuse, but Frodo has had enough and drafts him to become their guide. After he tries to escape, the Ring-bearer tells Sam to bind him with the Elven rope. The creature pitifully wails in torment at its touch and pleads for its removal. Frodo agrees on one condition. Gollum says he will promise anything the hobbit desires. He begs to see the Ring to bind his sworn word to it. Its present Bearer firmly warns him about the perils of such a thing. He knows it will only bring more harm to his shadow.

Frodo confirms the Ring, though hidden, is in Gollum's presence. With these words, Sam has a vision of his master as a "a tall stern shadow, a mighty lord who hid his brightness in grey cloud . . ." (*LotR* IV:1, 604). It cannot be a coincidence Frodo perceived Galadriel during her temptation to claim the Ring in a similar way. The gardener now sees how his master would appear if he did so.

Gollum swears to serve "the master of the Precious" (*LotR* IV:1, 604). Cleverly, he does not state exactly who this is.

After Sam removes the rope, both hobbits catch their first sight of Sméagol. The ruined hobbit's pleasure to have company again other than Gollum and the Ring knows no bounds.

> Every instant of time is in some sense timeless, for the choices made at every moment have the potential for changing the course of all future time and the meaning of past time. Pity, Mercy, Forgiveness are the qualities which make it possible to assume this about time: those driven by greed, possessiveness, hatred are tied irrevocably to the past Fall and to time. Frodo's act of mercy seems to touch something deep in Gollum, to remind Gollum that he might not be as bad as he has been. . . . (Mathews 39)

> Perhaps because Frodo treats him in a civil and polite fashion, Gollum begins to recover his freedom, his Sméagol self. Frodo calls forth Gollum's best traits by refusing to focus on his worst ones. Tolkien thus echoes what, in his *Confessions*, St. Augustine says about God's own love for him: 'In loving me, You made me lovable'. In response to Frodo's faith in him, Gollum begins to speak in the first person singular, and he swears never to let Sauron have the Ring - a promise that, in fact, he never breaks. (Wood, *Gospel*, 132)

Though Pope Benedict XVI does not speak of Frodo, his words apply to the Ring-bearer's compassion for Gollum: "Those who do not harden their hearts to the pain and need of others, who do not give evil entry to their souls, but suffer under its power and so acknowledge the truth of God [who cannot suffer but can 'suffer with' someone] - they are the ones who open the windows of the world to let the light in" (87).

Frodo's presence is a great balm to Sméagol, who has known naught but darkness and misery for centuries. Barry Gordon observes Aragorn is not the only one who shows kingship: ". . . it is also present in Frodo's dominion over Gollum. The latter's one hope of freedom from the evil that possesses him lies in obedience to the master he has set over himself" ("Kingship").

In turn, Sméagol-Gollum's presence in Frodo's life is a gift. Kerry Dearborn notes strangers are "to be seen as a means of grace" (139). Gildor, Tom, Goldberry, Glorfindel, Strider, Elrond, and Faramir are also conduits of this. The success of the Quest depends in part on the faith and trust the Ring-bearer shows in his willingness to have strangers guide him. Sméagol serves his new master as faithfully as he can and even begins to love this stranger he ultimately betrays and ultimately saves. Roger Sale remarks about the importance of the trio of hobbits who save Middle-earth:

> Here, in the instinctive wish to tame Sméagol rather than to destroy him . . . , is the seed of Frodo's heroism. Just as he could see the light in Aragorn's eyes and so discover a young but ancient lord, so he can look at the Gollum at his feet and see 'himself,' struggling to stay alive against powers insuperably great.
>
> . . .
>
> If neither [Sam nor Sméagol] is of anything like Frodo's stature, however, he is lost without them. But Frodo knows this and because he knows it can 'find' himself in his love for Sam and his compassion for Sméagol and his dependence on them. As long as he is thus dependent, and willingly so, the urge to possessiveness that lies at the heart of the Ring's power to destroy can be combatted. Frodo's virtue lies in his good manners, and his good manners are

his recognition of the blessed and cursed otherness of his servant and his wretched guide. (273, 285)

Light and Darkness

On the way to the Dead Marshes, Frodo offers Sméagol a bit of *lembas* beard. After the wretched creature chokes on it, the Ring-bearer reveals more of his spiritual growth with his insight into Gollum's sad state. He intuitively understands the bread would be a blessing to his shadow. He also recognizes it is too soon for such a being of darkness to tolerate such goodness. He has though fully embraced Gandalf's slender but present hope for Sméagol's cure. He hopes one day the ruined hobbit will become strong enough to take advantage of the grace the bread offers. The Ring-bearer knows something has happened within Sméagol's heart and soul. The exact nature and how long it will last remain mysteries to him. Stephen C. Winter provides a powerful meditation:

> Frodo longs to heal the great divide that lies between himself and Gollum but he cannot. For this to happen Gollum would have to come and 'Open his Grief' as the [Anglican] Prayer Book puts it. He would have to weep for the murder of Deagol. . . . He would have give up the fiction of the *birthday present* withheld . . . to justify his crime. He would have to acknowledge his utter wretchedness. He would have to long for healing, maybe even for death. He would have to give up the Ring and join Frodo and Sam in their wish to destroy it and all the evil that it has the power to do. ("Let Him Come"; emphasis in original)

The dwindling supply of food concerns Sam, but it does not bother Frodo. He sees no reason to fret about a future beyond the completion of the task. He does not think there will be one. But even though the Ring-bearer has doubts whether his strength will last, he remains unbowed to continue along his appointed path.

> Frodo has some faint hope that they may achieve their quest. That is no small hope. The fate of all Middle-earth rests on it, and it would be a great deed. But he seems to

have very little hope that he and Sam will survive the doing of it.

. . .

It seems Frodo cannot bear anything more than the quest. To keep hope alive with such a weight as the Ring is a task almost beyond imagining. To hope even for the strength to destroy the Ring is all that Frodo can manage. Sam, though, has a different kind of responsibility to bear. He doesn't have to carry the Ring, but he is committed to caring for Frodo. With less weight to bear for the quest, he can carry hope that he and Frodo may live. (Eagleson, *Wisdom: Two Towers* 45, 51)

The next day, Frodo and Sam follow Gollum into the nightmare landscape of the Dead Marshes. Without the creature to guide them, they likely would have bypassed the desolate area for the seemingly better route across the plain where Isildur defeated Sauron millennia before. Gollum confirms 'seemingly' is the operative word. Not long would they have remained free if they chose that road. Even if they chose the path through the Marshes, Frodo and Sam could have easily lost their way or drowned without their companion's slow but certain guidance. Thus appears another sign the One who chose Frodo out of all beings chose wisely: only hobbits could pass safely through because of their smaller weight. But this does not mean the Marshes pose no danger to them.

In a dream-like state, Frodo either falls or actively seeks out the bodies he sees underneath the water. Margaret Sinex notes:

Whatever Frodo's motivation, it is undeniable that the corpses and candles fascinate him most intensely. Further, he does not seem to share the extreme horror gripping Sam. Ominously, the power of the candles seems most potent for the Ringbearer.

Indeed, Frodo appears to have entered an altered state of consciousness while his companions have not. . . . These underwater candles induce a strange torpor as well as this physical paralysis. (101-102)

Frodo tells Sam what lies beneath: the fading fairness of the fallen Elves and Men, as well as loathsome orc bodies. Anna Smol and Sinex remark:

> The events in the passage of the Dead Marshes epitomize what is happening to Frodo throughout the quest: physically and psychologically, the boundaries of his self are disintegrating as he gets closer to Mount Doom. Frodo retreats more often to a world of sleep and dream, while his waking self finds even walking under the weight of the Ring more difficult. (Smol 48)

> Frodo and Sam resist the fascination of the candles and the temptation to sleep with the Dead. . . . yet . . . they are not unaltered by their passage. . . .
> To manage the Marshes at all, they must shed some of their hobbithood. . . . (Sinex 104)

Deep into the night, the hobbits reach firmer ground. Frodo and Sam have but a moment to enjoy the moon before another sight brings horror into their hearts. Gollum is certain the overflying Nazgûl knows of them.

Sam notes with concern how the Ring becomes a burden that grows heavier and heavier for his master. Frodo does not feel this merely as a physical weight. Even worse is the perception of Sauron's steady and malevolent gaze. As far back as Galadriel's Mirror and much more intensely at Amon Hen, Frodo senses this. In the Golden Wood, he perceived the truth his Enemy would not see him unless he willed it. But he has lost sight of this. He fears the Dark Lord traces each breath and step. Fortunately, while this is Frodo's perception of reality, it is not truly what occurs. Several days later, Sauron luckily begins to labor under false perceptions as well, as regards the identity and location of the Ring-bearer.

Normally Frodo and Sam relished any light, but not as they stand in the desolate land outside Mordor. ". . . unfriendly it seemed, revealing them in their helplessness - little squeaking ghosts that wandered among the ash-heaps of the Dark Lord" (*LotR* IV:2, 618). As such, they "appear much less likely to succeed in their quest. Thus this imagery of reduction offers another imaginative means of highlighting their impressive and poignant struggle against despair" (Sinex 107).

Sam wakes to hear Frodo's voice. But it is not the Ring-bearer who speaks. Ilúvatar or the Valar use the familiar sound to ensure the gardener hears the debate between Gollum and Sméagol about their lust for the Ring. Sméagol valiantly defends the promise he made and the master he made it to. But he cannot prevent Gollum's attempt to steal the Ring while Frodo slumbers.

The Ring-bearer wakes ignorant of this drama. Even in this diseased and desolate land, he received a dream he cannot remember but which provides a soothing balm to his heart and soul. He commends Sméagol for his fidelity and asks for guidance to the Black Gate.

The hobbits come before the Morannon and wonders how they will elude the ever-vigilant guards. Frodo knows he must go on. Gollum quickly points out the attendant perils of this and begs him not to continue. The creature offers two alternatives: keep the Ring or return it to him. But the Ring's present Bearer takes the charge laid upon him with the utmost seriousness. His determination to openly walk into the arms of his enemies distresses Sméagol to no end. He mentions again the terrible danger of continuing as Frodo intends and speaks of another path which will not pose such an immediate threat to the success of the Quest.

Before the Ring-bearer makes any decision, he looks down upon the vast armies at Sauron's call. He chooses to trust his guide once more. He recognizes his and Gollum's destinies are intertwined. Whatever evil intentions the creature first had, the Ring-bearer notes he has not followed through with them.

Frodo strongly admonishes Sméagol about the perils of Ring-lust and how the promise made by the Ring will likely doom the miserable being. He tells him in no uncertain terms never to entertain the fancy recovery of the Ring is possible. He chillingly prophecies the precise manner the ruined hobbit later dies.

Sam notes Frodo looks and sounds different than before. The gardener reasoned his master was nice to others because he was unaware of their faults. The Ring-bearer is not blind. He sees clearer than his gardener. "[Gollum] remained a human being, not an animal or a mere bogey, even if deformed in mind and body: an object of disgust, but also of pity - to the deep-sighted, such as Frodo had become" (Tolkien, qtd. in Hammond and Scull 447). He beholds both the wretched good within Sméagol and the evil within Gollum. In his desire to save Sméagol, Frodo warns him where such evil will bring him in the end. His harsh words come from concern for the creature's soul, but they frighten his guide badly.

Gollum details the path he used to escape the Black Land and which Frodo could use to enter it. The Ring-bearer challenges the veracity of his story, but he has an odd sense the creature does not wholly lie.

The Ring-bearer senses Gandalf's concern, but he is unaware of what he perceives. As he struggles with the evil choices before him, he wonders why he of all people must attempt to enter Sauron's realm. Still he has a task to remain faithful to. It is a doom he first chose in his own home and repeatedly as his Quest progressed. This acknowledgement does not help with his decision, but something else does. Sam's poem about an oliphaunt gives Frodo the grace-filled opportunity to laugh amidst his troubles. He makes up his mind and tells Sméagol he will risk the path the creature suggests.

Frodo and Sam follow their guide into Ithilien. Gollum chokes on its fragrant beauty, but the hobbits revel in it.

The gardener watches his master sleep and reflects upon the light which shines ever brighter from him. It overcomes the artificial youth the Ring gives and shows the true beauty of a middle-aged hobbit. Anne M. Pienciak notes, "While [Frodo] becomes weaker physically through the course of his trials, he also becomes stronger spiritually. A certain light seems to shine within Frodo, reminiscent of the description of saints" (20). Another admirer observes, "Frodo seems the embodiment of the gift that Galadriel gave . . . the light of innate goodness shining in the shadow of darkness and evil to light the way for others" (piosenniel). Sam professes his love for his master. As this is not dependent on whether the light is there to see or not, it remains true amidst the greatest darkness Frodo's heart and soul travel through.

The Ring-bearer wakes from "another gentle, unrecoverable dream of peace" (*LotR* IV:4, 641). After the hobbits enjoy their little feast of rabbit stew, the smoke attracts unwanted attention. The Rangers who come upon them are a blessing in more ways than one. The men keep the hobbits safe from the perils that surround them. It also results in one of the unexpected friendships Elrond predicted would come.

Faramir does not quite trust the hobbits at first, but he gives indications he will once he learns more. Frodo assures the Ranger captain any foe of Sauron would find an ally in him. The young man leaves the Ring-bearer and Sam with Mablung and Damrod. He then continues on with the other Rangers on the errand that brought them to this area.

Sam falls asleep and wakes to see Faramir in the midst of a rather harsh interrogation of Frodo. The Ring-bearer skillfully navigates these dangerous waters without revealing the nature of his mission. Faramir asks whether the hobbit was on good terms with Boromir. Frodo says he did extend friendship to the man. He tells nothing of how they parted.

> The episode with Faramir also shows us a new side of Frodo. . . . he has never had to face an interrogation of the sort that Faramir forces upon him. Frodo could easily escape Faramir's suspicions simply by stating the truth: that Boromir was a traitor who sought possession of the Ring himself, betraying the Fellowship. But Frodo refuses to admit the truth out of regard for Faramir's honorable memory of his late brother. Of course, Boromir was not completely evil . . . ; in this regard, Frodo may be attempting to pay tribute to his former colleague. But the fact remains that, in his conversation with Faramir, Frodo sacrifices his own comfort and honor to preserve the good memory of someone who betrayed him. The nobility of Frodo's act is impressive indeed. When we watch how well he holds up

under pressure from the accusatory Faramir, we develop a deeper respect for the hobbit's empathy and strength of character. (Gardner et al. 151)

Faramir shocks Frodo with news of Boromir's death. It was a sore enough trial to save the Ring from one man alone. What would happen now surrounded by so many if Faramir wished to trap him just as his brother attempted? Yet Frodo intuitively understands the young man is a better man than Boromir.

The Ranger captain tells Frodo of a strange experience he had almost a fortnight previously. From Faramir's detailed description, Frodo confirms the young man's belief he indeed saw his brother's body. But the hobbit thinks it was a vision or perhaps an illusion sent by Sauron. Faramir is convinced what he saw was true. Frodo remains unsure, but fears grow among his doubts whether the rest of the Company survived. He asks to continue on his doom-fraught path.

Faramir notes the "elvish air" about Frodo (*LotR* IV:5, 653). But even so, he states he cannot release the hobbits into the wild. He has standing orders to bring all strangers within the limits of Gondor to his father, Denethor, who will decide their fate. Rather than immediately obey this decree, however, he says he will take them to a Ranger refuge and there ponder what further role he will play in their lives.

On their way to Henneth Annûn, Faramir tells Frodo he knows the hobbit did not answer his questions completely. The Ring-bearer counters he did not mislead him and revealed everything he safely could. The young man compliments Frodo on how well he did. But he has read between the lines and guesses the Ring-bearer and Boromir did not get along very well either from the beginning or at the end. Faramir does not know what Isildur's Bane is, but he guesses it was the source of this ill will. Frodo admits the young man is close to the truth, but he does not say more.

Faramir guesses Isildur's Bane is some terrible weapon of the Enemy. He assures Frodo whatever it is, he has no desire to use it himself. He does not press the hobbit further about his task but to say he could perhaps help him with it. The Ring-bearer remains silent. He longs to tell Faramir everything, but he is not ready to trust him. He still vividly remembers the terrible lust and madness in Boromir. These scars have yet to fully heal. He fears what would happen if he reveals too much to the wrong person.

After they reach Henneth Annûn, Sam overhears Anborn's report to Faramir of a strange creature he thought may be a squirrel. He obeyed his captain's standing order not to shoot any animal without need. Though he knows it not, this man saved Gollum's life and the Quest.

After a large meal heartily satisfies the hobbits in body and soul, Faramir engages them in further conversation. Frodo still refuses to speak of the task before him. Instead he regales the Ranger with the Company's adventures, choosing to focus on Boromir's brave deeds. To the Ring-bearer's horror, Sam lets slip the secret of the Ring and what Boromir tried to do.

Faramir at last understands all Frodo held back. He faces his moment of temptation, but he passes the test his brother could not. He states Sam's accidental slip did not happen by unlucky chance but as part of a providential plan.

Faramir beholds Frodo in a new light and sorrows the hobbit came into such a burden. He holds great respect for him to withstand the temptation to use the Ring. He realizes he is in the presence of goodness and of a marked person who will suffer much for undertaking a task not of his own desire. He does not want to know anything more about the Ring, lest the temptation to use it himself overwhelm his prudent judgment and cause him to forsake his promise to refuse it. In this matter, he deems Frodo to have the greater strength.

Faramir asks the nature of the Ring-bearer's errand. Suddenly tired beyond measure, the hobbit reveals it and his doubt he will ever accomplish it. The Ranger catches him as he collapses.

Some hours later, Frodo wakes. Faramir draws his attention to a creature in the water. He asks the hobbit if the Rangers should carry out their duty to eliminate any threat to their hideaway's secrecy. After a slight hesitation, the Ring-bearer answers with a firm no and admits this is his missing companion.

Faramir states the steep price Gollum must pay for coming to the pool without leave. Frodo says the creature knows nothing of such an injunction or the penalty for violating it. He merely wants to have his favorite meal.

Anborn wishes to shoot. Faramir asks Frodo why the man should stay his hand. The hobbit gives several reasons. One contains strong echoes back to when Bilbo spared Gollum. Even the exact words could be used: "The creature is wretched and hungry . . . and unaware of his danger" (*LotR* IV:6, 670). The Ring-bearer also remarks Gollum's fate and the Ring's are somehow intertwined, though in which way he knows not.

Whether dead or alive, Faramir says Gollum must come into the custody of the Rangers. Frodo offers to do this and even offers his own life if he is not successful. David Mills notes, ". . . Frodo can be used by Providence not only because he is merciful but also because he submits to an authority [Gandalf] that asked for mercy" ("Writer").

The Ring-bearer moves cautiously, using all four limbs, like the creature he now risks his life to save. A mix of compassion and revulsion well up within the hobbit to hear Gollum and Sméagol talk. The latter speaks of the tasty food; the former rants about the loss of the Precious and his wish to murder the hobbits and Rangers. Frodo longs for freedom from both voices. A brief temptation crosses his mind and heart to take advantage of Anborn's desire to shoot. The Ring-bearer defeats it before it takes root. He reminds himself the broken creature is under his care, and he has a responsibility for his welfare. Not even Gollum's deadly intent changes this. Sméagol has done them no harm, so Frodo intends no harm to him.

The Ring-bearer pleads with his guide to come with him and warns him of the dreadful peril he is in. After Gollum balks, Frodo threatens to use the Ring against him. The hobbit realizes the end point of this venture, Sméagol in the hands of the Rangers for his own safety and theirs, will seem to the creature a terrible betrayal. Yet he knows of no other way to save his companion's life or of a way to explain he was not complicit in evil but meant his actions for good. Anborn and two other Rangers roughly subdue the creature.

The Ring-bearer tries to offer reassurance. Only over his dead body will the men do evil to Gollum. The creature spits at him in response.

As the men lead Gollum to Faramir, Frodo and Sam follow behind. The Ring-bearer feels completely miserable about what happened. He tells his gardener they must now live with whatever consequences will come from the inevitable and false conclusions their guide draws from his capture.

Faramir tells Gollum Frodo saved his life. But the man must know more before he does the same. The Ranger gives the Ring-bearer a knife to cut the creature's bonds. Gollum fears his master means further harm to him, but Frodo again asks for trust and pledges his support.

Gollum denies any prior knowledge of the Rangers' hidden cave. Faramir detects the darkness in the creature's heart and soul, but he discerns no lie. Gollum begs Frodo to save him and gives surety he will not return. Both the Ranger and Frodo accept this. The Ring-bearer speaks of his own oath to keep Gollum safe. He does not wish to betray his word. Faramir goes against the laws of his land and releases Gollum into Frodo's custody.

After Anborn takes Gollum away, Faramir begs Frodo not to follow the creature further. He tells of the evil he saw within. The hobbit defends his companion as not completely lost to darkness. Surely the man does not want him to break his word to keep the creature safe and accept his guidance? Faramir says he does not, but he admits he longs to give this exact counsel. He sees the wicked being only intends to bring Frodo to a bad end.

The Ranger captain tells of the dark rumors of what dwells near to Minas Morgul and the fell beings who occupy it. He pleads with Frodo not to travel there. The Ring-bearer presents a chilling alternative if he does not continue on his appointed Road. Should he instead take the Ring to Minas Tirith and have it wreak havoc there and ruin the Tower of Guard just as the Tower of the Moon was? Faramir has no answer to what Frodo should do in place of continuing forward to his doom. But his heart is not given over to despair. He desires to see the hobbit once more if by some miracle the Ring-bearer survives his perilous mission.

After Gollum reappears, the Ranger captain says the creature must wear a blindfold so he cannot give away the location of the hideaway. The Ring-bearer insists he and Sam wear them also, with his done first. He hopes this way Gollum understands the men intend no wickedness. Faramir counsels them which way to go and bestows kisses upon the brows of Frodo and Sam in farewell and blessing. Strengthened by this unexpected friendship and love, the hobbits continue on. Gollum says he has forgiven the Rangers and Frodo himself for his betrayal.

The hobbits follow their guide to the road that leads to what was once Minas Ithil. The road is empty, at least to physical eyes. Sam tries to buoy his master's spirits by quoting his Gaffer, just as Bilbo quoted his during his own arduous journey: *"where there's life there's hope"* (*LotR* IV:7, 685; emphasis in original).

The three come to the Cross-roads just as the sun peeks out before it sets. It blesses Frodo and the fallen head of the statue of one of the kings. Orcs defaced it, but flowers defiantly grow about it and make a makeshift crown. Akin to the star Sam will see in Mordor, Frodo glimpses the same truth here about the transient nature of evil. Bruce Palmer notes:

> . . . Frodo was touched with an unknown hope, a brief glimpse of things higher and more enduring than the realm of evil . . . .
>
> . . . Frodo and Sam had seen a poignant reminder that hope is found in the most unlooked for places, and at the most opportune time. (23-24)

But the Ring-bearer cannot stay in the land of kings. He must press ever onward into the Enemy's devouring darkness. He must forsake the light and face its death in his heart and soul, so it will still live for others.

The incredible evil which surrounds and emanates from Minas Morgul causes a terrible disorientation in Frodo. It drags him forward toward itself. He has no choice to obey, as though but a puppet with another will in control of his strings. Sam stops him before he can utterly betray himself and the Quest.

With a tremendous effort, Frodo masters his will again and resists the compulsion to flee to the Tower. The Ring tries to regain control, but it cannot compete with him and Sam combined. For a second time in the near presence of a Nazgûl, Frodo temporarily loses his sight. Sam helps him away.

The hobbits wearily follow Gollum upwards away from the Tower. Frodo begs for time to rest from overwhelming fatigue. "Weariness and more than weariness oppressed him; it seemed as if a heavy spell was laid on his mind and body" (*LotR* IV:8, 690). Gollum becomes so frantic to move on, even Sam agrees with him. The Ring-bearer at last stirs enough to make another effort, but he is only half-awake.

By this time, the hobbits and their guide can only watch a great number of their adversaries march forth. The wound Frodo received on Weathertop torments him. The Lord of the Nazgûl stops, as he detects his master's treasure somewhere nearby.

Another terrible battle of wills takes place. This time Frodo's does not collapse under the assault. Terror of discovery freezes him in place. He feels the weight of the coercive power beat against him again. But unlike Weathertop, Frodo has no desire to claim the Ring and chooses not to respond. He knows well now its treacherous nature. He also knows he is not strong enough to challenge his adversary with the Ring: "not yet" (*LotR* IV:8, 691). He would have never thought he could be if he had complete control over his desires and ambitions. Rather the Ring implants this idea and slowly warps his humble nature and infects it with pride.

Unable to breach Frodo's defenses by coercion, the Ring chooses to bypass them altogether. Here the Ring-bearer experiences another aspect of dissociation. Depersonalization is "Persistent or recurrent experiences of feeling detached from, and as if one were an outside observer of, one's mental processes or body (e.g. feeling as though one were in a dream; feeling a sense of unreality of self or body or of time moving slowly)" (*DSM* 272). The hobbit feels detached from his own body while he watches his hand move independently of his own will toward the Ring. He will also have an altered perception of time in Cirith Ungol before Sam comes to rescue him.

The force against Frodo wins the ascendency only briefly until his will beats it off. It directs his hand to grasp the Elven starglass and achieves victory over the terrible power arrayed against him. Once more triumph slips from evil's grasp within moments of its attempt to seize it.

Frodo feels no reason to celebrate. A more subtle attack wraps its tendrils around his heart. The utter futility of his task sinks him under a black wave. He blames himself for taking too long to defeat his enemies. Even if he could destroy the Ring, what would be the point? Who would be left to celebrate it? All peoples would already be under the Shadow.

Sam's voice calls his master from this pit of pride and despair. The latter continues to weigh the Ring-bearer down, but he no longer abandons himself to it. He smiles and recommits his mind, body, heart, and soul to his mission. With no longer any fanfare expected or wished for, Frodo's mind is set free to continue to do what he can, as long as he can. He holds the light-filled phial against his heart to combat the darkness that surrounds and penetrates it.

The hobbits and Gollum begin the long, tiring ascent up the Stairs of Cirith Ungol. At the top of the Winding Stair, they are within the sight of the Tower. The Ring-bearer feels if he can get past that, he will have the ability to fulfill his task. To successfully complete one completely unlikely thing makes the next one seem easier.

Sam longs for his and Frodo's adventures to appear in a story begged for during a long winter's night. He thinks there will be a clamor to hear about how valiant his master was. The gardener's musings provide the Ring-bearer once more the grace of hearty laughter, not just once, but twice. Philip Gibbs notes this kind of mirth gave WWI soldiers "an escape from terror, a liberation of the soul by mental explosion, from the prison walls of despair and brooding" (qtd. in Garth 44). Frodo acknowledges the critical aid of his beloved guardian. He is certain readers will want to hear all about his humble gardener.

After Sam's suspicions about Gollum rise again at the creature's absence, Frodo shows no concern. If the miserable being has betrayed them, there is nothing they can do about it. He does not think Gollum went to arrange this, but he allows some kind of villainy is likely afoot. He guesses Sméagol continues to make a true attempt to save the Ring from Sauron. But the Gollum part awaits the proper window of opportunity to claim the Ring for himself. As Frodo sleeps peacefully in Sam's lap, their love continues to combat the hell of their journey.

Upon Gollum's return to this tender scene, Sméagol shows himself for the last time. Frodo's compassion and kindness gave him the strength to stand up to Gollum after centuries of being cowed and abused by him and the Ring. Gollum hates the light that occasionally comes through the prison they share. For Sméagol, this and his "scarred and beautiful" (Sale 287) relationship with Frodo are the only glimpses of the outside world he has. At the point his prison door opens its widest, at the moment of Sméagol's greatest exposure and vulnerability, he reaches out in love to Frodo. "This is Sméagol's finest moment, and so, by implication, it is Frodo's finest moment too. Beyond friends and kin, old and tired, Sméagol loves the specialness that is Frodo's care of him. . . . the tentative unbelieving response to a caring so unlikely it seem heroic even to the Gollum" (Sale 286-87).

Unfortunately, Frodo cries out in his sleep and wakes Sam. The gardener misinterprets Sméagol's fragile gesture. His harsh words shrivel the tender shoots of hope and love the Ring-bearer nurtured. They shatter Sméagol's last opportunity to return to the light Frodo gently coaxed him toward. Sam witnesses the ancient hobbit's death, but he does not know it. Gollum at last gains complete control over the mind, will, heart, body, and soul he so long shared. Tom Hillman notes a clear parallel between Sméagol's last moments and the tormented creature Bilbo recognized and fled from in the goblin tunnels:

> What Bilbo saw beneath the Misty Mountains, we see as in a mirror on the Stairs of Cirith Ungol. In *The Hobbit* Bilbo, poised to commit murder out of fear, glimpses the hobbit that Gollum was, and turns to pity. In *The Two Towers* Gollum, also poised for murder, sees in Frodo what he

himself has lost to the Ring . . . and nearly repents. But he stumbles against the pitilessness of fearful, watchful Sam, and 'withdraws himself'. As Bilbo leaped forward, Gollum fell back.

. . . [These two episodes] work together to reveal the razor's edge between murder and repentance, between pity and pitilessness, between leap of hope and lapse into despair. ("Gollum")

Frodo wakes and greets Sam with a smile and Sméagol with concern for his well-being, unaware Sméagol is no more. He asks if he and Sam can proceed on their own now. If so, he will consider the creature's vow fulfilled.

But Gollum is not ready to leave them just yet.

The treacherous creature leads the hobbits to the foul entrance to Shelob's Lair. Just as Frodo feels 'naked in the dark' in the depths of Mordor, he is also here: completely vulnerable and exposed to the enemy who waits within. John Garth notes, "In the lair of Shelob, enemy of light and beauty, of freedom, hope, imagination, and inspiration - the central impulses of Tolkien's mythology - Frodo encounters another cloud of terror . . ." (46).

The sense of touch flares and fails. Hearing lessens but is not lost entirely. Smell remains in agonizing intensity. The hobbits force themselves to go on, as time stretches into a terrible eternity. In the forbidding darkness, they come upon an opening where they sense a malignant evil. Only ever so slowly can they force themselves to move away until "suddenly it was easier to move, as if some hostile will for the moment had released them" (*LotR* IV:9, 703). Frodo calls out for Sméagol, but he does not receive a response.

As they continue, the Ring-bearer and Sam hear a terrible hiss behind them.

Crucible

Sam receives the inspiration to remember Frodo carries Galadriel's phial. He calls upon his master to use it against their ever-approaching enemy. "For a moment it glimmered, . . . and then as its power waxed, and hope grew in Frodo's mind, it began to burn . . ." (*LotR* IV:9, 704). The Ring-bearer marvels at the power of this awe-some gift. He responds to the inspiration to call upon Eärendil "and knew not what he had spoken; for it seemed that another voice spoke through his, clear, untroubled by the foul air of the pit" (*LotR* IV:9, 704).

None of this impresses the hobbits' adversary. By the light of the phial, they see their foe for the first time: a demon in the form of a gigantic spider. Indeed, the mother of those Bilbo encountered in Mirkwood. Frodo and Sam flee, but their enemy follows. The Ring-bearer realizes the uselessness of retreat and makes a brave stand against their foe. Alison Milbank likens this time as akin to Dante and Virgil's time in Hell from *The Divine Comedy*:

> . . . with the help of good memories of Tom, Galadriel, and even of Elbereth Gilthoniel, [Frodo and Sam] face up to the nothingness that Shelob embodies. . . . Before Dante and Virgil can leave Hell they must pass Dis or Satan, who is stuck in the hole at the bottom of Hell and is completely monstrous and horrible. . . . The effect on Dante is extreme: 'How chilled and faint I turned then, do not ask, reader, for I do not write it, since all words would fail. I did not die and I did not remain alive; think now for thyself, if thou has any wit, what I became, denied both life and death.' The nonbeing that Dis causes is like that of Shelob in that he is a literal blockage to thought and life. . . . Dis is like Shelob also in that he does not kill outright but eternally chews his prey, just as she slowly poisons and devours her victims: Frodo is caught between life and death like Dante's narrator. The way out for Dante, advised by Virgil, and Frodo by Sam, is to engage with Satan and not to run away.

It is for Dante necessary to grasp Dis's hairy flanks and climb down his body. Similarly that is how Sam deals with Shelob, by facing her and not turning tail, engaging her bodily. (78)

Shelob is no match for the Ring-bearer's courage. As he advances, she retreats and flees. This snack has teeth she did not expect. After Sam celebrates this great victory, the hobbits attempt to make their escape. They come so close to the exit, they feel the outside air. Frodo still senses Shelob's malicious will. He uses Sting to rend the tremendously strong cobwebs that block their path. Drunk with the ecstasy of freedom, the Ring-bearer runs from the tunnel.

Frodo urges Sam on, but the gardener does not feel only the heedless gladness his master does. He watches Shelob speed toward the Ring-bearer. Gollum grabs the gardener. Frodo remains ignorant of the terrible danger about to overwhelm him.

Sam fights off his assailant and mounts a ferocious assault on his master's after Shelob strikes Frodo down. Her wickedness is no match for the gardener's love. After she flees, he rushes to his master. Fury overwhelms him after his desperate efforts to wake him prove vain. After this burns through the hobbit, he looks at his master and remembers he saw this scene before.

As Sam has no way to bury his master's body, he does his best to honor it. He talks to Frodo as though still alive. He know he must leave, but this is a terrible choice to make. He holds his master's hand, as he debates with himself the best reason to depart. It comes to him the only thing worth leaving his master's side for is to fulfill the Quest. He does not think it his place to promote himself to Ring-bearer. He realizes he is not the one who made this decision: the same One who chose both his masters now chooses him. Sam kisses his master's brow and takes the Ring from around his neck. Frodo does not react in the least. The gardener promises to return if at all possible and die by his side. Judith Klinger observes:

Although Sam's 'one wish' . . . assumes suicide, or willed death, upon his return, death is now envisioned as a 'quiet rest' that Sam can eventually share with Frodo, and a reunion that affirms an irrevocable bond. This re-interpretation of death takes the shape of a wish, replacing the earlier 'black despair.' Emotionally, Sam overcomes death as loss and terminal separation. But his wish also manifests an intuitive comprehension of Frodo's true state, contradicting surface appearances. ("Hidden Paths" 188)

Sam fully takes upon the terrible weight of the Ring. He looks at his master by the light of the phial. ". . . in that light Frodo's face was fair of hue again, pale but beautiful with an elvish beauty, as of one who has long passed the shadows" (*LotR* IV:10, 716). A short distance away, he looks back again one last time. Klinger remarks about this profound time for him:

As uncertain as the 'glimmer on the ground' may be, a reflection of combined grief and hope, it also translates a new insight into external reality, first glimpsed by the light of the Phial when Sam took his leave. . . . This ambiguous perception of Frodo transcends the stark opposition of life and death, and perhaps more significantly, extends to a previously unimaginable future: a point in time when Frodo's passage through the shadows of Cirith Ungol, through apparent death and the trails of the Quest, will have slipped into the remote past. ("Hidden Paths" 189)

Sam is not far away when he hears orcs discover Frodo's body. He chases after them, but he cannot catch them before they carry his master away. Even Gorbag notices the Ring-bearer's Elvish air.

Sam's will is not the only one at work here. His first choice to leave, so agonizingly reluctant and second-guessed, is the correct one. So is his decision to draw the farewell out as long as he did. It positions him far enough away from the orcs to avoid capture himself, but close enough to hear news which stuns him beyond belief. His master is alive!

Sam rushes after Frodo. But again, he is too late and providentially so. What seems disaster is not as the orcs unknowingly aid the Quest another step further. The Ring-bearer enters the Tower of Cirith Ungol the only safe way he can: unconscious and in the arms of his enemies. Stephen C. Winter notes another element of this divinely used moment:

> If it had not been for the orders that the orcs received from Sauron they would have left Frodo to die by the roadside or played with his body like a football. As it is The Dark Lord is concerned about news that someone has penetrated his defences and so gives some attention to the matter. His greater attention is given to the armies that he sent to overwhelm the defences of Gondor or else it would not be orcs that he would have sent to the pass of Cirith Ungol but something more trustworthy that would have carried Frodo straight to his presence. As it is the orcs carry Frodo just far enough . . . ("Shagrat")

Sam mounts his rescue of Frodo with an enormous amount of courage and grace. After a terrifying search through the Tower of Cirith Ungol proves seemingly vain, he does not give up. He responds to the inspiration to sing and reaches his master, just beyond the moment he feared him lost forever. Tom Shippey notes the last two lines of Sam's song, "I will not say the Day is done, / nor bid the Stars farewell" (*LotR* VI:1, 888) are to "encourage Frodo in his prison not to lose hope" (*Author* 203).

Frodo responds faintly to his guardian's song. Snaga opens up the trap-door and climbs up into the hobbit's prison. The gardener races after him to stop his whip from scoring the Ring-bearer's flesh a second time. Sam rushes to his master's side and takes him into his arms. Frodo marvels to see him. Sam assures him they are truly reunited. The class distinctions of master and servant, older and younger hobbit, have become increasingly meaningless as their ordeal deepens. Indeed from this moment they are reversed.

Frodo relaxes and sleeps in the shelter of Sam's arms and love. Ralph C. Wood notes their friendship is a thing of exquisite beauty, even holiness.

. . .

Their mutual regard is also akin to the friendship of Jonathan and David: 'the soul of Jonathan was knit to the soul of David, and Jonathan loved him as his own soul' (1 Sam 18:1). (*Gospel* 135, 136)

John O'Donohue speaks of the depth of St. Patrick's friendship with God. It also perfectly defines Frodo and Sam's blessed bond and the strength it gives them:

> *Anam* is the Irish word for soul and *cara* is the word for friend. The *Anam-cara* is the Friend of the soul. This is one of the most beautiful concepts in the Celtic tradition. An ancient affinity and belonging awakened between two people in the *Anam-cara* relationship. This relationship cut across all other connections. In your *Anam-cara* you discovered the Other in whom your heart could be at home. The depth and shelter of this *Anam-cara* belonging enables Patrick to endure the most awful conditions (10).

Sam wishes he could spend eternity in such a blessed embrace of his master, but he knows he cannot. Frodo wakes and wonders where they are. He tells his beloved friend of the traumas he suffered after Shelob struck him down and the orcs revived him. He speaks for the second time about terrible dreams but does not mention their nature. Frodo is sure he will forever remember the torment he endured. Sam agrees, especially if he keeps reminding himself of it. The gardener does not understand how talking of trauma can help the victim. Frodo, however, intuitively recognizes its healing properties, despite the nature of hobbits to speak little of ill things.

In the glare of a red lamp, Frodo looks "as if he was clothed in flame" (*LotR* VI:1, 890). The Ring, the fire of Ilúvatar's love, and the hobbit's own love for Middle-earth consume him ever more.

After Sam asks what their next step is, the knowledge the Quest is lost crushes Frodo. There is no way now to outrun the doom soon to fall. The gardener reveals a second marvel. Wonder overcomes the Ring-bearer, but it quickly turns to a terrible possessiveness and demand to return the fell object. Sam first makes an offer to share its burden. He does not say this because he lusts for it himself, but from pity and compassion for his master.

Frodo does not see this reality. He is naked in all ways: physically, spiritually, morally, and psychologically. A terrible vision of an orc comes before his eyes and obliterates his faithful Sam. As in a mirror, he sees his own lust for the Ring. He grabs it back from the enemy who stole it from him. His gaze is void of all love he bears for Sam. "This is the Ring's corruption in its most devastating mode" (Rutledge 325). But it cannot break the bond between the hobbits. Sam's love swallows Frodo's hate and meets his aggression with a broken, forgiving heart. It absorbs the stabs made and forms again an impregnable barrier against it. As the haze of Ring-induced rage burns away, it leaves Frodo devastated it took such hold of him, just as it left Boromir. Indeed, man and hobbit lament their lapses with identical words: "What have I said? What have I done?" (*LotR* I:10, 390; VI:1, 891). The Ring-bearer begs his beloved Sam for pardon.

This time of torment is terrible for Frodo, both to endure, but also terrible in the power it brings him to fight his interior battle against the Ring.

> In some ways he's weaker afterward, depending more on Sam for help, as if something in him had been broken. But if something had been broken, something else had gained strength. Before [Cirith Ungol], the Ring can tempt Frodo. . . . After Cirith Ungol, the Ring seems to have lost the ability to tempt him and instead tries to batter him into submission. . . . Frodo's loss of everything in the Tower brought him to the point where he was wise enough, and spiritually mature enough, that the Ring had nothing left to tempt him with. (Shaw, "They've taken")

Frodo again demonstrates the astonishing ability of hobbits to recovery quickly from trauma. He teases his faithful guardian about whether Sam remembered to check into the availability of lodging along their path to Mount Doom.

The Ring-bearer offers an insightful observation about the nature of evil and its limited powers: "The Shadow that bred [orcs] can only mock, it cannot make. . . . it only ruined them and twisted them . . ." (*LotR* VI:1, 893).

Frodo gives Sam the *lembas* crumbs he gathered. He says not to worry about obtaining more water, for what hope is there they will even see the next day?

The hobbits leave this terrible place of torture become a sacred space with their reunion. As they come near the gate, they feel the malevolence of the Watchers. Frodo collapses as a debilitating weakness comes him. In Sam's hand, Galadriel's phial shines out. He responds to the inspiration to call to Elbereth, and Frodo repeats part of what he said in Shelob's lair. The combined power which flows through their voices shatters not only the Watchers' ability to hold them back but collapses part of the Tower.

The Ring-bearer and his faithful companion flee for their lives. They take a blind jump in the dark from a bridge moments before enemies race across it. Frodo discards the heavy orc-mail Sam found for him. He already carries two terrible weights: hopelessness and the Ring. Another is too much. Neither affect his will to continue. Frodo gives the first hint of his loss of memories in his admittance he can no longer recall home. Sam says a prayer to Galadriel for light and water.

Light comes first, likely through the intervention of the Valar. Excitement grips Sam, as from far off, he sees clouds break and realizes Sauron suffers a setback. The next time a Nazgûl cries out, it does not freeze their blood as it had previously.

Sam draws fresh hope from what he sees. What little the Ring-bearer receives is not enough to sustain him. If something wonderful happened, it is not near enough to help them. They must move not closer to it but further away. He refers to the Ring for the first time as a fiery wheel. This hellish vision is ever before him and colors all his perceptions.

The Vala Ulmo is likely who answers Sam's second prayer. The hobbits come upon the miraculous sight and sound of water which traveled far to cross their path and strengthen them. Sam says he wants to drink first, for better he to discover it deadly than Frodo. Though buried increasingly in darkness, the Ring-bearer's heart still receives light from the Powers which protect him. He intuitively realizes the water could be a grace-filled gift instead.

Nightmares plague Frodo's sleep. Though his heart and mind find no peace in either rest or waking, his body recovers some strength to continue in the dim light that passes for day.

As the hobbits look down upon the vast orc camp amidst a blasted landscape, Frodo speaks again of his despair for any success in their Quest. Yet in the next breath, he tells of his determination to do everything possible before their enemies inevitably apprehend them. He defiantly opposes the Ring, even as its claws rend his heart and soul. He does not try to stop this desolation by actively beating himself against it. Such would only strengthen it. He moves on to spite it and in spite of it. This inner battle, Constance G. J. Wagner notes, is "the true War of the Ring - the War Within. This is a spiritual battle, fought with spiritual weapons . . ." ("War" I:338).

Frodo and Sam pass by a small orc encampment but see no one. Only until they are several miles away do they hide after they hear two orcs argue. One tracked their scent, but lost it after Gollum fouled it up by taking the orc-mail the Ring-bearer discarded. This simple action done from fatigue has such far-reaching effects, it could be argued had Frodo continued to wear the armor his mission could have failed. Yet he did not and so all unknowingly allows grace to use his weakness. The armor not only throws off the tracker, it also saves Gollum's life by deflecting an arrow shot at him.

Frodo gives Sam custody of Galadriel's phial and bequeaths Sting to him as a gift. He retains an orc weapon, but he intuits he will never use it.

The next morning, the hobbits decide their only option is to tread upon an orc-road. The Ring-bearer once more admits his despair, but again refuses to bow to it. In another reversal of who is master and who is servant, Frodo asks Sam to take charge of where they will travel. His words make clear the success of the Quest hinges on the gardener's constant support to strengthen Frodo's own stubborn will to continue. This is Sam's vocation: to be Hope-bearer for the Ring-bearer. He helps his master in his spiritual battle by fighting his own.

> Loss of hope is a tragic side-effect of the isolation of psychological abuse: loss of hope and insidious doubt that anything will ever change or improve. Frodo doubts himself in this way as he gets further into the unfamiliar and intimidating environment of Sauron's stronghold. When all of Frodo's sense of efficacy is drained from him, he can only follow Sam blindly toward their destination. (Wilkerson 89)

Even though the torment Frodo suffers "nearly has his soul ripped from his body" (Smith 175), Sam notes his face is "content and unafraid" (*LotR* VI:2, 907). An extra serving of *lembas* strengthens the Ring-bearer's instinctive knowledge he is in the best hands he can be: Sam's and the One who chose him. The beginning and end of a poem from Dietrich Bonhoeffer applies to Frodo's peace:

> By faithful, quiet powers of good surrounded
> so wondrously consoled and sheltered here
> . . . .
> By powers of good so wondrously protected,
> we wait with confidence, befall what may.
> God is with us at night and in the morning
> and oh, most certainly on each new day. (*Letters and Papers* 528-529)

At nightfall, the hobbits travel upon the perilous orc-road a good distance before seeming doom falls upon them. An enemy company marches straight toward them. Frodo loses his faith in luck, but Sam has not. The orcs unwittingly draw their disguised foes into the fold. For the Ring-bearer, this is a catastrophe. He has no choice but to muster his strength to continue toward whatever terrible fate awaits him.

Sam, however, waits for eucatastrophe. And it comes. Just as orcs unknowingly aided the Quest by carrying Frodo into the Tower of Cirith Ungol, they help enable its success again here. The hobbits travel safely through the most dangerous part of their journey at the punishing speed of a forced march, shielded within an enemy army, which they could not have passed by any other way without discovery.

Yet even Sam begins to despair of a successful end to their toil as Frodo's strength falters. But, as before in the Tower, what seems the end of all hope is but a step away from the threshold of victory. The orc-company the hobbits are embedded in providentially arrive at the same time as other hosts at a cross-roads near one of their camps. Sam takes full advantage of their natural propensity to battle each other to escape with Frodo.

The hobbits continue to toil toward their goal for four more days. They endure the terrible assault of Sauron's malice which pervades the land. Sam sees signs of the terrible battle that rages within his beloved, silent master. He notes Frodo does not always seem aware of what is in front of him. He observes him raise his hand to defend himself from invisibles foes. Other times Sam watches it move toward and then away from the Ring. Clyde Kilby observes:

> I think also that the element of will in the Tolkien story rises above that of simple Stoicism and takes on something at least of a Christian color. Frodo's heartfelt commitment to the cause does not save him and Sam from increasing need to command their wills as they move deeper and deeper into enemy territory. Their whole way through Mordor is that of dedicated hearts careless of their own safety except as that safety pertains to the fulfilling of their purpose. As they neared Mount Doom, the weight of the Ring and the steadily increasing desire of Frodo to use it as a means of escape became a battleground in his inner parts and forced him over and over to will against the easy way. One of the powers of the Ring is by destroying selfhood to bring the user into the dominion of Sauron, to turn him from a being

into a wraith. One of the clear evidences of Frodo's increasing greatness of character is his steady will to resist incredible temptation in the face of growing physical weakness. Saint Augustine's doctrine of the effective will is well illustrated by Frodo. (138-139)

Judith Klinger agrees: "In Mordor, where the Ring's power is greatly increased, the struggle to control his own hand becomes emblematic of his continued insistence to uphold the distinction between himself and the Ring" ("Fallacies" I:363). Douglas Charles Rapier and Constance G. J. Wagner also speak of this horrific ordeal:

> Every hour of every day, [Frodo] was subjected to the unrelenting malevolent manipulations and enticements of the Ring. He knew no solace after Gandalf's fall in Moria. He had no refuge after his sojourn in Lórien. The Fellowship did not assuage his disunion from the world of light which had begun with his wounding on Weathertop. Frodo was alone in his thoughts with a demon spirit, the spirit of Sauron the Deceiver. Waking and sleeping, he strove with the will of the Ring for control of his own will, his own spirit, his own life and the lives of all he held dear. That he was able to maintain control over himself despite the other-worldly power of Sauron's Ring until that momentous moment at the Cracks of Doom is astounding considering all those who had been overwhelmed by it. (Rapier I:298-299)

> . . . all that [Frodo] was, is, and ever will be on Middle-earth is laid upon the altar of the Quest.
>
>   . . .
>
> By giving *of* himself, by giving *up* himself, Frodo has saved all others from a fate worse than death - from slavery and darkness and suffocating despair. (Wagner, "War" I:340, 342; emphasis in original)

Sam ponders the power of *lembas* bread to strengthen their wills to bear the unbearable. Water is the other critical element to their survival. Only the risk of the road gives them the opportunity to come upon a foul but blessed source left for the enemy troops to use.

Even though the gardener knows how his master will react, compassion stirs him to offer to carry the Ring once more. Frodo utterly rejects his guardian's lovingly generous offer. He recognizes how close to the edge he is: "I am almost in its power now. I could not give it up, and if you tried to take it I should go mad" (*LotR* VI:3, 916).

Sam suggests he and Frodo discard everything unnecessary to the completion of their Quest. The Ring-bearer throws away much of his orc-gear. He knows they are useless in the war he fights. Rather he wields love, courage, loyalty, pity, mercy, and forgiveness as his weapons. He knows those held by the heart can prevail where those held in the hand cannot. Sam parts with his beloved pans. "Symbolically, they seem to be stripping themselves to the core of their humanity: the indomitable will to carry on to the end" (Pienciak 119).

Despair continues to ravage the Ring-bearer, but it still cannot destroy his will to continue. He willingly endures the torment as it brands him. But it does not own him. He recognizes it as the bully it is and does not allow his aggressor to feed on fear to enhance itself. Rather, he starves it by embracing it. This is not a surrender to its power but a path to resistance of it. The words of Dietrich Bonhoeffer reflect Frodo's actions:

> The only way to overcome evil is to let it run itself to a standstill because it does not find the resistance it is looking for. Resistance merely creates further evil and adds fuel to the flames. But when evil meets no opposition and encounters no obstacle but only patient endurance, its sting is drawn, and at last it meets an opponent which is more than its match. (157-158)

The Witch-king threatened to take Éowyn to the houses of lamentation and expose her to the Eye. The Mouth of Sauron will speak of drawing out Frodo's torment as long as possible before returning him, broken in mind and body. Both are present realities for the Ring-bearer. This is a awful place to be for its grave cost but also an awe-ful place. Only through the power of grace and love does Frodo endure the self-shattering of his harrowing journey. He bears the withering of his heart and soul without complaint so others may live. He does not hide from the reality this has the ability to crush him. But he does not let the assault of evil hide from the fact he has the power to crush it. "Frodo is painfully aware that his task is hopeless, but instead of inducing him to give up, his despair actually motivates him to continue. Endless miles of noxious swamps, barren wastelands, and rugged mountains don't weaken his resolve; neither does exhaustion, hunger, or thirst" (Virginia). The Ring-bearer expects to die at the end and so moves forward in complete freedom and detachment.

After Sam asks his master if he recalls the rabbit in Ithilien, Frodo says he has no memories of anything from nature. "No taste of food, no feel of water, no sound of wind, no memory of tree or grass or flower, no image of moon or star are left to me. I am naked in the dark, Sam, and there is no veil between me and the wheel of fire. I begin to see it even with my waking eyes, and all else fades" (*LotR* VI:3, 916). Frodo's spiritual gift to discern the nature of people underneath any guise extends now to the 'soul' of the Ring and of Sauron. It is "as if he could now only see the Ring's power, its essence, as it might look without the materiality of its golden surface" (Hallam 36).

Stretched out upon this burning wheel, the Ring-bearer does not will to move from it. For even though the One Ring scars and consumes him, the Secret Fire of the One, Eru, consumes him as well as a freely offered holocaust offering. His self is a candle which he allows to burn down until there is nothing left. Thomas Finch's words perfectly apply to Frodo's trial: "The only possible way to move through these days is through the grace of God and the strengthening of the Holy Spirit" (113). Verlyn Flieger movingly notes, "With a degree of self-abnegation matched only by Gandalf's surrender of himself in Moria, Frodo goes beyond evil, beyond self, beyond physical or mental wholeness to be completely broken down in order that he may be remade. He is splintered light . . ." (*Splintered* 158).

Millennia before St. John of the Cross writes about the dark night of the soul, Stratford Caldecott and Trudy G. Shaw note Frodo takes this mystical journey. "The Carmelite spirituality of the 'dark night' seems particularly appropriate for Frodo in Mordor, and that blind despair in which he staggers toward Mount Doom, no longer able to visualize or remember light, or fresh water, or any natural beauty" (Caldecott 92-93).

> After the passive night of the senses in Cirith Ungol, Frodo seems to be dropped almost immediately into the active night of the spirit. . . . Both Frodo and the Ring have grown, and their battle becomes constant - and more deadly. There will be no end to it until one of them is destroyed. . . .
>
> The complete stripping of identity that Frodo experiences would . . . be worse than death, because even beyond death we remain who we are. And Frodo's loss doesn't take place in one 'heroic' moment but through a halting, gradual process he has no way of stopping except by giving in to the Ring's evil and abandoning his task. As his very selfhood is consumed by the Ring . . . Frodo can only watch as he continues to allow it to happen. But, the all-important fact is that he *does* continue to allow it to happen rather than give in to the Ring. . . . There's no passivity in this dark night . . . .
>
> In *The Ascent of Mount Carmel* . . . John's 'nothing'/'not' (*nada*) means giving absolutely everything over to God:

> To reach satisfaction in all
> desire its possession in nothing.
> To come to possess all
> desire the possession of nothing.
> To arrive at being all
> desire to be nothing . . .

> To come to the pleasure you have not
> you must go by a way in which you enjoy not.
> To come to be what you are not
> you must go by a way in which you are not . . .
>
> . . .
>
> The process isn't complete yet . . . but [Frodo] knows
> only too well what's happening to him and what the end of
> that process will be, and yet he continues to doggedly use
> every bit of will he does have to force his way toward exactly
> that end, still trusting that he's being led by whoever or
> whatever it was that called him to the task, and still carrying
> the hope that goodness and beauty will endure even if he
> can never know them again. ("naked in dark"; emphasis in
> original)

Stephen C. Winter notes the difference uses of darkness
between Sauron and his mighty adversaries:

> Sauron is the ultimate example of one who in seeking to save
> his own life loses it. Frodo and Sam walk freely into a
> darkness knowing that it is likely that they will lose their
> lives. Indeed Frodo fully expects that he will lose his life and
> it is possible that by this point he even looks forward to
> death as a kind of release. For Frodo and Sam the darkness,
> an experience that they have not chosen yet, in so far as they
> able, they have embraced, is the road to life, both to the
> world that they will save and to themselves. ("Sauron")

The hobbits' torture continues, as the air itself labors to stop
them. Yet as their mortal strength pours out, immortal grace pours
in to honor and fortify them. The words of Friedrich Nietzche apply
here: "He who has a *why* to live for can bear almost any *how*" (qtd.
in Frankl 104). Sam toils for Frodo; Frodo struggles for all Middle-
earth. Sauron's greatest peril is not at the Black Gate, as he believes.
Rather, it inches toward him with the instrument of his defeat. So
mighty are the hobbits' fortified wills, in a more modern age, if the

Dark Lord bombed their location, before the smoke even clears, he could but watch his unstoppable opponents rise from the crater covered in dust and blood and continue on.

Frodo sleeps in Sam's arms the final night of their Quest. In the morning, the Ring-bearer has no strength to walk further. But he still has the will to continue. As his legs can no longer serve him, he uses his hands and knees. Before he gets far, Sam lifts his master up and marvels at the small weight, even with the Ring. Edith Crowe notes "at this point they are essentially one being, with Frodo carrying the spiritual burden and Sam the physical" (7). Grace and love gives Sam the ability to do this.

But even a beloved child can become heavy. By the end, exhaustion reduces the gardener to a crawl himself before his strength temporarily reaches its end. Frodo expresses his gratitude after they stop. Near them is Sauron's Road, the direct path to the Cracks of Doom. It serves now as an instrument of the Dark Lord's doom. Grace reaches out to the hobbits once more. They rouse to answer an urgent interior prompting to continue without delay.

Frodo crawls onto Sauron's Road with Sam. The Ring-bearer feels a coercive force turn his gaze toward Barad-dûr. He sees the terrible Eye for an instant before clouds cover it once more. "Frodo at that dreadful glimpse fell as one stricken mortally" (*LotR* VI:3, 921). Again, the overwhelming compulsion comes upon him to claim the Ring. He still wills to resist, but he realizes he can no longer do this on his own and whispers to Sam for aid. Anna Smol notes, "Although Frodo is not taking a stand with sword drawn as he did at the Ford of Bruinen, his attempts to prevent his hand from touching the Ring even when he has lost autonomy over his own body must be acknowledged as an immense effort of heroic will" (53).

Sam holds Frodo's hands as though in prayer and blesses them with a kiss. The Ring-bearer does not fight to get away from this tender grasp. What was irresistible a moment before fades before the great force of the gardener's love. Judith Klinger notes, "Through the portrayal of mutual love and trust between Sam and Frodo, Tolkien casts the Ring's limitations into sharp relief. It cannot comprehend love of an Other for his own sake" ("Fallacies"

I:365). Sam carries his master once more up the slope. The lucky scarcity of lava aids them.

But here, so close to victory, another peril strikes the hobbits. As Gollum desperately attacks Frodo, evil again brings about good it does not intend. The threat to the Ring and to the Quest calls forth from its Bearer a fierce energy to protect them both. He grasps the Ring and warns Gollum of the creature's impending end. He also gives his rival, shadow, and mirror one last chance to escape. But it is too late for the ruined being.

At the nadir of Frodo's physical strength, he shines the brightest spiritually, "imbued with mythic splendor . . ." (Hein 206). The Ring-bearer is aware only of the devouring darkness, but grace grants Sam sight of both the brightness of his master's soul and the fire which seeks to destroy it. Throughout the Quest, from Rivendell, to the Emyn Muil, to Ithilien, to Cirith Ungol, to this moment, it gives the gardener visions it grants to no one else. As in the barrow, as at Amon Hen, as soon to come in the Sammath Naur, the Quest stands on the knife-edge with Frodo balanced between good and evil. From the Ring comes a voice which prophecies Gollum's doom if the creature dares to fight Frodo for it again. The vision fades, and Sam sees his master nearly spent from his terrible ordeal.

But the Ring-bearer no longer crawls. Grace gives him a final burst of strength to walk upright toward doom. He says goodbye to his beloved guardian. He told him as they discarded their gear, they would need nothing at the end of the Road. Frodo now leaves even Sam behind. He has nothing left but his will to complete his task.

Broken

Sam now has the chance he has longed for: to get rid of Gollum for good. But the same insight Bilbo and Frodo gained into the creature's wretched soul now enlightens the gardener's heart and burns through his rage. It stays his hand as it had his masters'. Gollum pretends to take advantage of his pity and command to leave. Once Sam turns his attention back to Frodo, the ruined being follows behind.

Volcanic eruptions provide the only illumination within the Chamber of Fire. By this hellish light, Sam spies his master. C. Baillie observes, "[Frodo] walked, staggered, crawled through the valley of the shadow of death. All the way through Mordor, his will – his desire to stave off Darkness - was what kept him plodding, one foot after another. That will held firm right up to the last moment. Then he came to the end of that hell-march and there to welcome him was the son of the morning" ("Frodo and Grace"). Lucifer was named so, and no, Morgoth is not at the Fire, but his greatest servant is.

Earlier drafts of this section of the tale show in fascinating detail the actual temptation Frodo faces, as the Ring compels him to claim it. Just outside the Sammath Naur, ". . . Frodo suddenly feels, many times multiplied, the impact of the (unseen) *searching eye*; and of the enchantment of the Ring. . . . He hears or feels a deep, slow, but urgently persuasive voice . . . ." This offers him all manner of things up to and including a share in the power of the Ring, if only he waits for the Nazgûl and returns with them to the Dark Tower. This frightens the hobbit greatly. As on Amon Hen, "He remains immovably balanced between resistance and yielding, tormented, it seems to him a timeless, countless, age." But when he comes to himself this time, there is no voice to counsel him against folly. "Then suddenly a new thought arose - not from outside - a thought born inside *himself:* he would keep the Ring himself, and be master of all. Frodo King of Kings. . . . He would make great poems and sing great songs, and all the earth should blossom, and all should be bidden to his feasts" (*Sauron Defeated* 5; emphasis in original).

This vision appears in keeping with the love of story and song Frodo and Sam share. But as it comes from the Ring, it would turn to great evil and result in the destruction of the Ring-bearer's humble hobbit nature. The outwardly peaceful appearance is false. This new Lord of the Rings would not be a glorified Mayor benignly overlooking a great feast. The earth would not blossom long.

At the same time Éowyn speaks of feeling as though she stands upon the edge of an abyss, Frodo truly does. As Gandalf and Aragorn fight at the Black Gate and men willingly give their lives in the blind hope of aiding the hobbits, the Ring-bearer stands at the brink of "the spiritual abyss into which Sauron has fallen ages earlier" (Rosebury 37).

As the Ring consumes Frodo, its Bearer can battle it no more. He said yes to Ilúvatar many thousands of times with each painful breath and step. There is now but a strand of will that can no longer speak. Sam calls out to his master. Frodo's voice answers, but it is not Frodo who willingly says the terrible words the gardener hears next. The Ring-bearer who long toiled in torment to keep from happening what is about to can no longer prevent it. Barry Gordon notes, "Towards the end of the quest, Frodo is left with only the capacity to will. . . . Then, when the moment comes for the actual destruction of the Ring, the theme of self-negation in sacrifice reaches its highest point: the ability to will is taken from him" ("Kingship").

Sam hears Frodo's voice fling aside the Quest and the victory he and Sam nearly died to achieve. Tom Shippey remarks, "It is . . . interesting that Frodo does not say, 'I choose not to do', but 'I do not choose to do'. Maybe (and Tolkien was a professor of language) the choice of words is absolutely accurate. Frodo does not choose; the choice is made for him" (*Author* 140). This aligns with Tolkien's thoughts: "I do not think that Frodo's was a *moral* failure. At the last moment the pressure of the Ring would reach its maximum - impossible . . . for any one to resist, certainly after long possession, months of increasing torment, and when starved and exhausted" (*Letters* 326; emphasis in original). Verlyn Flieger notes, "His use of *choose* and *will* makes it clear that he believes he is acting freely. But the negative, the repeated *not* is telling evidence that his will has been perverted and his choice pre-empted" (*Splintered* 153-154; emphasis in original). Michael Martinez adds:

> Frodo gives in to the Ring at last, but it has taken months of demonic torment to drive Frodo to claim the Ring for his own. The claim is not born of pride and arrogance, nor of ambition to become a great and powerful lord. It's essentially an act of insanity, an insanity brought about by the breaking of his mind. Frodo is in many ways reduced to the stature of an Orc who has had his free will stripped from him, his choices denied him. (431)

The weight of Sauron's dark power crushes the created, but it has none over his Creator. The Dark Lord is but a servant himself, serving a greater evil, just as the hobbits serve a greater Good. Morgoth wove evil into the Great Music from the beginning. It was also part of the fabric of Middle-earth from the time of its creation. Ilúvatar could have changed this, but He allowed it to continue to show it had no power over Him and His designs. He overcomes Sauron's might in the hobbits' weakness. The Ring plays a part too in its own destruction. Frodo, Sam, and Gollum are the vessels to get it there.

> Frodo deserved all honour because he spent every drop of his power of will and body, and that was just sufficient to bring him to the destined point, and no further. Few others, possibly no others of his time, would have got so far. The Other Power then took over: the Writer of the Story (by which I do not mean myself), 'that one ever-present Person who is never absent and never named' (as one critic has said)" (Tolkien, *Letters* 253).

Even if Ring-bearer and Ring-destroyer is thought by others and by Frodo himself as one and the same, they are actually two different missions in the mind of Ilúvatar. Frodo's was to create a setting where the end of the Ring could come about (*Letters* 326).

This he does perfectly. His will holds to the end of his task. Once he fulfills it, the Ring overwhelms him.

But too late to save itself or its master.

Gollum smites Sam as the knowledge of what Frodo just did smites Sauron. The gardener wakes to see the wicked creature battle an invisible adversary.

> That Frodo and Gollum both freely participate in the Ring's destiny to arrive at the Cracks of Doom shows *their* free will collaborating with *its* fate. *Doom* and *choice*, *must* and *will* are interlocking systems, cogs turned 'by small hands' which move the wheels of the world while 'the eyes of the great are elsewhere'. . . . The final confrontation at the Cracks of Doom brings the conflict down to a contest of 'small hands' - Frodo's hand now wearing the Ring and Gollum's. . . . (Flieger, "Music" 34-35; emphasis in original)

The two Ring-bearers seem evenly matched until Gollum's sharp teeth decides things. "Frodo has done all in his power, but the salvation of the world is beyond that power. Such salvation can only come through a combination of human effort and the Grace of God" (Crowe 7). After the hobbit claims the Ring and is claimed by it, Ilúvatar claims him back.

> Above and beyond the intentions and purposes of all the characters in the saga stands an overarching Power whose purposes will not fail, but whose workings quietly exist outside the conscious awareness of created beings. Its greatest strength is realized through human weakness. The presence of such Power is glimpsed in the text such as . . . Gandalf's statement . . . to Frodo that he was meant by a Higher Power to possess the Ring. The sudden transfiguration of Frodo in his struggle with Gollum just prior to the Ring's destruction further attests to the presence of the supernatural in league with the good. . . . It is, therefore, hardly accurate to call it Fate, as some scholars

tend to do. It is the power and purpose of God. (Hein 208-209)

Ecstasy over possession of the Ring so overcomes Gollum, he does not watch his step. Gandalf's intuition the creature had his own role to play comes to fruition. Gollum began his ownership of the Ring by theft and ends it so. But many instances of grace through pity come between to save Middle-earth. Sam's is the most important because it is last. If he did not show it, all the others, and the entire tortuous ordeal to get to the Mountain would be in vain. Love gets Frodo to the Fire; hate and lust get Gollum there. Sam stands in between them. Part of his role was to extend love in the form of pity and mercy to the hated Gollum. This saves Frodo from a terrible fate. With the Ring's terrible power to "devour" and "possess" its Bearers (*LotR* I:2, 45, 46), Shippey notes, ". . . this will not be just a physical take-over. The Ring turns everything to evil, including its wearers" (*Author* 114). Indeed, Sam's love and Gollum's hate save Middle-earth from a hate far stronger than Gollum's, but not as mighty as Sam's love for Frodo, Frodo's for all Middle-earth, and Ilúvatar's love for them and their world. Stephen C. Winter notes these free choices to extend pity give grace the opportunity to operate:

> It is Gandalf who realised that in the long, violent and malicious history of the Ring only Bilbo took it without violence and only Bilbo gave it up freely. Grace takes Bilbo's kindly disposition, a very small thing in the great scheme of things and puts it to world-transforming use. Grace perfects Nature and so opens the door to Frodo's pity for Gollum and Sam's realisation that he too cannot kill Gollum, much as he wished to do so. And it opens the door to Gollum's last attack upon Frodo and his fall into the Fire with the Ring [i]n his grasp. Without all these small things the Ring could not have been destroyed. Grace would have had no door by which to enter the story. Grace cannot achieve perfection without Nature. ("Gollum")

Marion Zimmer Bradley remarks Gollum's fall into the Fire, "glossed as an accident of his exaltation, is more, far more, than accidental. . . . In 'saving' his 'precious' from destruction, he *genuinely* saves Frodo, whom he loves as much as he hates, from destruction too . . ." (123; emphasis in original).

As Mount Doom begins to collapse, Sam rescues his beloved master from the cataclysm, just as Gollum unwittingly delivers Frodo from other terrible fates. Tolkien noted if Gollum was not there, Frodo most likely would have jumped into the fire with the Ring. Another considered possibility was if the hobbit still managed to have custody by the time the Nazgûl came, they would pretend homage to him and take him outside the Cracks of Doom. While he fantasized about what he would do with his newfound power, the wraiths would destroy any chance of the Ring's destruction. If its Bearer had not gone completely mad and had the strength to refuse to go to Sauron, the Dark Lord would come to him (*Letters* 330-332). "Frodo would have been utterly overthrown: crushed to dust, or preserved in torment as a gibbering slave" (*Letters* 332). Luckily, the Ringwraiths arrive at Sauron's command only to have the volcanic ruin of their master's seat of power overcome them.

Even surrounded by the violent death throes of the Dark Lord's bid to dominate the world, Sam feels great happiness to see his beloved master no longer tormented by his terrible ordeal.

Frodo reminds his beloved guardian of Gandalf's intuition about Gollum's destined role. His next words may sound puzzling: "But for him, Sam, I could not have destroyed the Ring" (*LotR* VI:3, 926). But Frodo did not destroy the Ring. He had nothing to do with its end.

And everything to do with it.

If not for the Ring-bearer's embrace of his awe-ful destiny, Sam and Gollum could not have fulfilled theirs. Without Gollum's cursed and blessed presence, the hobbits could not have succeeded. And, as Frodo already noted, Sam is just as essential. If any one of these faltered, the Quest would have failed. All that happened - the betrayals, hunger, thirst, numbing exhaustion, all the myriad sacrifices willingly and lovingly made in the midst of horrific suffering - took place to remove the scourge of Sauron. "In the end perhaps the greatest threat to the evil of Sauron is not men at arms, but rather the bonds of love that kept the Hobbits from letting their friends fall into darkness and despair" (Smith 141).

Frodo shows an amazing capacity to forgive the one who betrayed him and saved him and all Middle-earth. He asks Sam to do the same. ". . . Frodo and Sam's calm discussion of Gollum's actions in the light of the destruction around them hints that a greater, unknown power of good is protecting them" (Gardner et al. 246).

The Ring-bearer is at peace and accepts his life will soon end. Trudy G. Shaw notes, "At 'the end of all things,' Frodo had given everything he could: physically, mentally and spiritually. . . . there was nothing left for him to willingly surrender. He'd already reached a spiritual level that many of us won't attain this side of death" ("all is dark").

Sam is not yet ready to surrender to the inevitable. His hope sustained them both for so long. Frodo gently tries to convince his dearest friend he need not hope further. Sam will have none of it. He must follow his heart and the hope he carries as a light to guide them. His gardener's hands and heart spent many years nurturing living things. This includes his master. He convinces Frodo they should move away from the worst of the apocalyptic destruction. Sam's hope receives its reward at the last moment.

After the gardener wakes in Ithilien, a voice he thought he would never hear again greets him. Gandalf blesses the hobbit with laughter. Frodo wakes to join them in their mirth. The wizard escorts the hobbits to the king. Aragorn genuflects before them to reverence their survival of such a brutal and black Road. Sam is overcome by tears of joy, as he hears a song in commemoration of the Ring-bearer's journey. Stephen C. Winter notes a connection between this and the Hall of Fire: "Once again we are taken back to Frodo's experience in the halls of Elrond when Bilbo's signing of the Tale of Eärendil and Frodo's experience of the mighty river of the Music of the Ainur all became one thing for a moment" ("Day").

Gandalf returns the items found on Frodo after the orcs captured him. The Ring-bearer marvels to see these long-lost things, but he does not want to reclaim the sword. Only after Sam insists, does he wear Sting. Michael Livingston remarks, "The lingering trauma of his experiences destroying the Ring is already beginning to prey upon his still-fragile mind" (84). Stephen C. Winter remarks:

> In part Frodo's refusal to carry a sword is a recognition of his own sense of failure. In another it is a desire on his part to have no more to do with war. Frodo has seen at first hand the horror of war, the malice and hatred that Sauron sought to unleash upon the earth, and he hates it.
>
> But Gandalf knows that the feast is not for Frodo alone nor is the magnificent raiment with which he is arrayed. When a great gift is received with grace it is not just the one who receives who is honoured but the one who gives as well. The circlet of silver which which Frodo is crowned, the sword with which he is girt, the mithril coat and the Elven cloak . . . are all an act of doing honour to those who gather at the feast. Some are great knights of Gondor, or of the Dúnedain, or of the guard of the King of Rohan. . . . when Frodo is arrayed as a fellow warrior and sits to eat with them he does them honour. He declares that their deeds in the war, their hopeless march to the Black Gate, perhaps achieved by overcoming great fear, are all worthy of honour. He names them brothers by sitting among them. And it is not just the warriors who are gathered at the feast who are honoured thus but every village, every family from which they have come. ("Frodo Gets Ready")

The Ring-bearer and his faithful guardian spend the following days revisiting some of the places they were while on their Quest. They do this "without fear and contemplate it in a way far beyond that which those who have not known the dark as they have done can do. This is the dawn that awaits those who watch through the dark of the night, the Springtime prepared for those who have endured through Winter" (Winter, "Frodo and Sam").

At the end of April, the entire host comes before Minas Tirith, where a great crowd waits to welcome them. Ioreth's fantastical version of Sauron's fall at the hands of two hobbits shows the historical facts have already grown into legendary proportions. With this and the minstrel's lay, Fleming Rutledge notes this "instantaneous conversion of Frodo into a figure of legend prepares us for the burden he must increasingly bear as he reflects upon the discrepancy between his failure at the Cracks of Doom and the heroic story that has been constructed around his journey" (350).

Faramir announces the return of the King to the great acclaim of the people. Fully aware who made this day possible, Aragorn asks Frodo and Gandalf to participate in his coronation. There is joy, but as Rutledge notes, this tale "is not a 'happily-ever-after' story. It is a story of cross-bearing, and therefore a story of wounds, scars and loss. . . . Frodo . . . is more damaged than anyone seeing him resplendent at the coronation could have known" (355).

Another tell-tale sign not all is well with Frodo is his remark upon sight of Arwen. The hobbit, who once fearlessly loved to walk under stars, speaks now of fear of the night. But he adds her arrival banishes them.

In mid-July, Frodo comes to see Aragorn and Arwen. The King feels unable to give any boon to equal the Ring-bearer's accomplishments. The Queen bestows two. Amy Timco notes, "Because, like Frodo, Arwen has given up her former life, she shares a special bond with the emotionally wounded Frodo after the Quest is completed. . . . Her unique status as a now-mortal Elf allows her to understand Frodo's displacement in a world to which he no longer belongs" (40). She also knows some wounds are incurable except by leaving Middle-earth. She sees in Frodo's silent agony tears in his soul similar perhaps to those of her mother. Centuries earlier, Celebrían was so deeply hurt by the servants of the Enemy she fled West to seek healing there. No mortal could receive a greater boon, but Arwen leaves it open for the hobbit to embrace or not. Judith Klinger notes, "The grace bestowed on him is no easy gift, nor is it portrayed as a pleasant escape from the burdens of mortality" ("Hidden Paths" 205). The Ring-bearer keeps this secret from his companions. In the depth of his own torn heart and in the breadth of his growing pain, he ponders the same choice Arwen had whether to stay or leave. Tolkien notes some of Frodo's thoughts of the possibility of going West: "Such a journey would at first seem something not necessarily to be feared, even as something to look forward to - so long as undated and postponable. His real desire was hobbitlike (and humanlike) just 'to be himself' again and get back to the old familiar life that had been interrupted" (*Letters* 328-329).

The fears Frodo spoke of but did not name to Gandalf upon the Arwen's arrival also prompts the Queen to give another rare gift: a white gem to aid the hobbit to combat the terrifying memories of his nightmare journey.

The hobbits return to Rivendell in time to celebrate Bilbo's 129th birthday. Two weeks later, Frodo and Sam sense an interior prompting to return home. The gardener loves Elrond's house for all it offers, but he wants to be back in the Shire. The Ring-bearer points out the one thing this Elven haven lacks: the Sea. Even now he longs for it.

Frodo and his companions come to say goodbye to Bilbo. After he gives them each gifts, the ancient hobbit asks about the Ring. Desire for the fell object still entangles his heart. Frodo tells him he has it no more. Bilbo thinks this is a shame, but then he remembers this was the whole point of their separation months before.

Content fills Bilbo to know his own adventures are over. He sings the Road song again, but changes a word in the beginning. He does not say "down from the door where it began," but "out from the door" (*LotR* VI:6, 965). William Reynolds notes the significance of this change:

> That he makes the change at this point is natural; during a period of confusion like that at the end of the Third Age, travellers who suddenly encounter dangers whose very existence they had never before so much as imagined would naturally think that the Road was taking them to disaster. Only when Bilbo has reached the very edge of Time and is preparing to leave it can he acquire a new perspective. The Road cannot threaten, he recognizes, because each of its seeming dips is ordered to assure the traveller of rest and safety at the finish of his course. The Road, History, events

in this world are all means, not ends. History is not an engine dragging individuals to destruction but the sum of individual reactions to situations involving choice; if the choices are rightly made, each individual is sure of his end -- returning properly to the Eternity that lies behind History. (15)

Bilbo is near the end of his Road and asks Frodo if he will edit the tales which he has transcribed and translated. The Ring-bearer promises to do so. The next morning before the hobbits leave, Elrond imparts a blessing upon Frodo. He tells him privately he will one day see Bilbo within the borders of the Shire. The Elf-lord does not give a specific date this will happen. But later, Frodo knows precisely when and where to greet his beloved uncle.

Seeking Rest

Janet Brennan Croft states, "One of the grimmest lessons *The Lord of the Rings* teaches about war is that some of the mental wounds it causes never heal in this world. Frodo is Tolkien's prime example of the heartbreaking effects of war on certain minds" (133).

While on the Quest, Frodo suffered several physical wounds, but the relentless mental traumas cause the deepest harm. Even before he reached Bree, he faced threats from the Black Rider and the barrow-wight. The Morgul-wound he received on Weathertop placed him in deadly peril. More blows followed from the Watcher in the Water and Gandalf's death to the shadowy but real danger of Gollum's pursuit of the Company. Lothlórien offered a respite, but Galadriel's Mirror also revealed the Eye of Sauron actively sought him. The orc attack on the River Anduin, Boromir's fall to the lure of the Ring, the terrible struggle on Amon Hen, the search of the Nazgûl, the intense sense of vulnerability and naked exposure to the ever-present Eye, the stress of not knowing at first whether Faramir is trustworthy, the malevolence and sting of Shelob, the capture by orcs and whippings in Cirith Ungol, the unwitting re-capture, and Gollum's assault inflict more damage. These multiple traumas meet Criteria A for post-traumatic stress. The *DSM* defines this as "[e]xposure to actual or threatened death [or] serious injury" either by "[d]irectly experiencing the traumatic event(s) [and/or] [w]itnessing, in person, the event(s) as it occurred to others." Criteria B requires the trauma(s) be relived through dreams, flashbacks, or "[r]ecurrent, involuntary, and intrusive distressing memories . . . ." Another element is "Intense or prolonged psychological distress at exposure to internal or external cues that symbolize or resemble an aspect of the traumatic event(s)" (271).

As the hobbits and Gandalf begin their return to the Shire, the psychological damage from these unhealed wounds becomes more apparent. Frodo suffers his first anniversary illness on October 6, the night of his first wound. He must force himself to cross the Ford of Briunen. He shows no awareness of his companions or surroundings. Though N. Duncan Sinclair does not speak of the hobbit, his observations about the intensity of flashbacks apply:

> Physically, emotionally, and spiritually the old moment [the original trauma] is relived, not just remembered. The unconscious cannot tell time, and when it projects the [trauma] onto the present moment, the time is both *then and now*. During some of these instances, the present is dimmed to the point where it is actually lost for periods of time. This is not a loss of reality, as is experienced in certain forms of mental illness. Rather, it is an experience of being captured by a past reality come to life in the present moment. (53; emphasis in original)

After Gandalf inquires, Frodo admits his physical and mental distress. He also wonders about his homecoming. He notes the Shire will be different because of the changes in himself. Tolkien notes, "That was actually a temptation out of the Dark, a last flicker of pride: desire to have returned as a 'hero', not content with being a mere instrument of good" (*Letters* 328). The Ring-bearer names his wounds and wonders where he can go to find peace from them.

By the end of the next day, Frodo returns to the present. He is so full of cheer, it seems he has no memory of the time he wandered lost in the past. His unease returns as they near where the Witch-king assaulted him. Criteria C includes "[a]voidance of or efforts to avoid external reminders . . . that arouse distressing memories, thoughts, or feelings about or closely associated with the traumatic event(s)" (*DSM* 271). Frodo shows this in his desire not to wear a sword after he woke in Ithilien, his great reluctance to cross the Ford, and his refusal to look upon Weathertop.

Once Gandalf and the hobbits reach Bree, Barliman Butterbur drops dark hints about trouble in the Shire. He expresses his confidence it is nothing the hobbits cannot handle.

On the way to the hobbits' homeland, the wizard announces he will leave them to see Tom Bombadil. He reinforces Barliman's faith in their ability to deal with whatever mischief is about. As they come to where the hobbits parted ways with Tom, Frodo desires to see the strange being again. Gandalf says now is not the time for it, but perhaps one day the hobbit may come to call.

After the wizard departs, Merry notes the group is now back to the number it began with. He remarks all their adventures seem dream-like, but now they are awake. Frodo disagrees. The wakeful time has passed, and he is sleepy once more. They all had incredibly intense experiences. Frodo's were the most beautiful and most terrible. For him, to return home is as unreal as a dream. He wishes to regain the peaceful life he had before. But this does not come true in Middle-earth. ". . . he has given too much of himself to the struggle to cast away the curse, suffered too much in the achieving of this peace for others" (Bradley 125). Verlyn Flieger adds, "Worst of all, he has lost the Ring he carried for so long and that has left its indelible mark on him. . . . Its loss cannot be made up, and Frodo is bereft of more than a finger" (*Interrupted Music* 142).

After all the privations and soul-lacerating pain Frodo willingly endured for months so his beloved home would remain safe, he returns to find it as violated as he. He and his companions arrive at the Brandywine Bridge after dark and encounter a gate and guards where none were before. After a night in the dismal guardhouse, they set out for Hobbiton to see for themselves who or what causes all this nonsense.

The leader of the Shiriffs says he will take the four hobbits to Bywater for judgment and then to the Lockholes. The Travelers laugh out loud at this ridiculous attempt to stop them. After Frodo announces his intention to continue, the Shiriff allows this, but he wants Frodo to remember he is under arrest. The Ring-bearer notes he will perhaps pardon the insult.

Once Frodo and company reach Bywater, they see terrible devastation to *smials* and gardens. *The Green Dragon* is no longer a place of welcome but the abode of ruffians. These try to intimidate them, but the hobbits have seen and endured too much for the men to frighten them. Indeed, Pippin threatens to use his sword after one of them insults Frodo. Sam and Merry back the tween up, but the Ring-bearer himself remains still.

After the men leave, Frodo lays out what their next step should be. Lotho may have started this whole mess but lost control over it. Before the Quest and such violation by evil, the Ring-bearer could not have grieved for his despicable cousin. His ordeal, however, gives him a viewpoint no untouched hobbit can understand or even imagine. His growth in pity and compassion moves him to mount a rescue mission. He acknowledges the possibility they may even have to go to battle to accomplish this. He commands no one is to die at their hands, if at all possible.

Merry says a fight is inevitable. In fact, he plans to start it. He raises Hobbiton while Pippin returns the next day with more aid from Tookland. Frodo again calls for no deaths on either side. The only exception he allows is to stop any of the intruders from harming the Shire folk. Merry agrees, but he tells his cousin, deaths may still come. "[Frodo] was not in modern terms a 'pacifist.' Of course, he was mainly horrified at the prospect of civil war among Hobbits; but he had (I suppose) also reached the conclusion that physical fighting is actually less ultimately effective than most (good) men think it!" (Tolkien, *Letters* 255). The Ring-bearer works to prevent any unnecessary losses of foes who surrender. "Frodo's transformation after Mount Doom defines his role in battle here. . . . Frodo acutely understands the need for mercy and redemption as someone who has profoundly experienced them" (Eagleson, *Wisdom: ROTK* 99).

After the defeat of the ruffians, the Four Travelers go up to Bag End to settle matters with the Chief. In Frodo's choice not to take Merry's advice to be harsh with Sharkey, he teaches his most powerful lesson on pity, compassion, and mercy. Saruman appears at the entrance of Bag End and gloats about the destruction he brought against the hobbits in payment for his loss of Isengard. Frodo sorrows for the ruined wizard.

The Ring-bearer commands the fallen Maia to leave. Some of the other hobbits cry for his death instead. Saruman counters their wrath with a threat the Shire and any hobbit who dares assault him will be forever ruined. Frodo calls the corrupt wizard's bluff and forbids any retribution against the fallen Maia. He knows the folly of vengeance will not solve anything. He again commands

Saruman to leave. As the wizard begins to obey, he attempts to murder the hobbit, but the *mithril* coat foils the effort. It almost costs Saruman his own life, as other hobbits push him down, and Sam readies to slay him.

Rather than react with like violence, Frodo orders his enraged gardener not to avenge the attack. The Ring-bearer exhibits once more the spiritual discernment of souls he showed with Strider and Sméagol. He sees the grace and light Saruman once possessed and responds with honor and respect for the Maia's lost greatness. He knows he cannot help him regain it, but he wants him to have the opportunity to seek it elsewhere. "[Frodo] will not deal out judgement in death, knowing that if Saruman dies in such rage his life as a wizard will have indeed come to nothing—and perhaps worse than nothing . . ." (Wood, "Frodo's Faith"). ". . . Frodo, in his encounter with Saruman, displays the grace and forgiveness he has learned from Gandalf, from Sam, and in dealing with Gollum" (Gardner et al. 240). Clyde Kilby notes Frodo's compassionate treatment of Gollum and Saruman "surpasses the norm of ordinary morality. It has the quality of such as Portia called 'an attribute of God himself'" (137). One knows even if the corrupt Maia succeeded in his assault and Frodo's lifeblood poured out, the hobbit's last words would still forbid retribution. He has indeed become "wise through experience," as Tolkien remarks Frodo's name means (*Letters* 224). "Only someone who has experienced redemption personally could act as Frodo acts in the later part of *The Return of the King*. If Frodo destroyed the Ring himself, perhaps he wouldn't understand the need for forgiveness and redemption as deeply" (Eagleson, *Wisdom: ROTK* 99). Stephen C. Winter adds:

> Frodo's own story has been one of profound self discovery and he has learned the pity of which the 14th century mystic, Julian of Norwich speaks when she tells us of the God who "looks upon us with pity, not with blame". He remembers the horror of Boromir's transformation through his lust for the Ring, of the first encounter with Gollum when he realises what he would become if he gave into it and the

journey through Mordor in which he tastes the endless living death that is the hopeless end of all its slaves. ("Saruman")

Rather than accept Frodo's grace and mercy as intended, it enrages Saruman. The wicked wizard understands the terrible wounds evil inflicted on the hobbit did not embitter him or turn him to darkness. His endurance of them filled him rather with the grace and light the fallen Maia himself already abandoned. Saruman once more refuses the antidote to evil and responds with his bitterest hatred yet. He detests Frodo for taking away the pleasure of harming the Shire. As one who once held great power, who is an incarnate angel, Saruman cannot abide he lives because a mortal stays the hands of those who would harm him. Jigyasa Mishra observes, ". . . Frodo defeats him, not by any weapon, . . . but by his kindness and courage. . . . We cannot expect Saruman to heed any other's hobbits words" ("Hero"). Trudy G. Shaw makes an even stronger statement:

> [Frodo] not only commands Saruman to 'Go at once,' but also to 'never return,' both necessary elements of an exorcism. . . .
>
> . . . In his quest for power, Saruman threw away the grace that Frodo has gained by not seeking power. . . .
>
> . . . Saruman recognizes legitimate authority (which, in Tolkien's cosmos, can ultimately come only from Eru), stronger than his own broken power, and yields to it. The spiritual strength we originally saw in the barrow has reached a new level. Which would mean - in the view of both Tolkien and John of the Cross - not that Frodo had gained more personal power, but that he had become a more open conduit of the power of God. Another way of imagining it would be to say that the transparency first noticed by Gandalf in Rivendell has increased: the glass has become more clear, allowing the Light to show itself more brightly. ("for I shall not be")

Frodo offers mercy and freedom from thralldom to Wormtongue. The man does not have the fortitude to accept this undeserved but freely offered gift. Saruman reveals how wicked his slave is and thinks he still has him under his control to abuse at will. Too late, he learns he does not. After Wormtongue murders his merciless master, hobbits kill him before Frodo can intervene to stop them. They watch as the Maia's spirit rises from the body it robed itself in. The Valar reject it from ever returning home. Frodo's pity for the fallen wizard continues, as he covers the remains.

The next day, the Ring-bearer helps release prisoners from the Lockholes. He brings Lobelia back into the light in more ways than one. She surrenders ownership of Bag End and leaves Hobbiton. To learn after her death she left him money to aid hobbits who lost their homes deeply touches him.

The hobbits work hard to restore beauty to their land. In time it heals of its wounds, but Frodo does not. He warned his fellow hobbits about the power of Saruman's voice to tell lies, but is he deceived himself? Does he believe the wizard's prediction about a short life full of illness? A sense of a foreshortened future is symptomatic of post-traumatic stress. Karen Milos notes this is

> Saruman's last act of vengeance, an attempt to destroy Frodo by planting seeds of doubt that would grow and choke off what little hope Frodo yet clung to.
>
> Saruman was a deceiver. . . . he perceived Frodo's unspoken fears and griefs as a point of weakness and shaped his deception accordingly.
>
> . . . Saruman, having failed to stab Frodo with his knife, resorted to stabbing with words that could not help but insinuate themselves into Frodo's vulnerable mind, haunting him and magnifying every memory and every pain into a portent of doom. (19)

Sam carried his beloved master up the Mountain, but he cannot carry him back down. Nothing and no one in Middle-earth can. Frodo left the land physically, but he remains trapped there emotionally and psychologically. Ben Murnane compares the Ring-bearer's trauma with those who suffered in WWII:

> . . . for some the burden they carried is too great to set down in this life. . . . Although in a sense, he saw less fighting than any of his comrades, Frodo's war burden is the greatest. The Ring-bearer suffered the most sustained contact with evil on his journey, but he also carried the responsibility of success or failure in the whole war: a single soldier's burden multiplied infinitely. (15)

Farmer Cotton witnesses the Ring-bearer's first March illness. He discovers the hobbit "lying on his bed; he was clutching a white gem that hung on a chain about his neck and he seemed half in a dream" (*LotR* VI:9, 1001). The farmer hears Frodo lament the loss of the Ring, whether he grieves and lusts for it in the present, or he relives how horrific it felt to wake in the Tower of Cirith Ungol and find it gone. "After suffering the tortures of the damned . . . for what seemed a veritable eternity, he still desires the Ring? Such is the measure of its superhuman grip" (Rutledge 367). It was an agony for Gollum to snatch the Ring from him. He was in the dark before, but at least the wheel of fire was a source of light. Now he does not even have that. He longs for the Ring just as keenly, if not more so, than Bilbo and Sméagol. But he does not have the hope they had to see it again.

The last time Frodo lay "half in a dream" was on the way to Rivendell after his knife wound. The description of his state of mind is identical. Both times the hobbit loses his grounding in present reality and wanders half-unmoored to another dimension or time, as one would in a dream.

While Frodo's first illness in October took a couple days to recover from, this second one starts on March 13 and only by the 25th is any recovery mentioned. It is not stated how long the Ring-bearer remained lost in his nightmare memories. He keeps this illness secret from Sam, who returns on the first anniversary of the Ring's destruction. Paul Kocher notes, "During the rest of his days [in] Middle-earth Frodo remains torn between the newly contending elements of his nature. . . . since [the Ring] came close to mastering him, he is still in the power of its memory. He still loathes it and longs for it after the fashion of Gollum. Here Frodo's propensity to dream is a curse because he cannot forget the 'precious' even in sleep" (119). Tolkien notes it is because of this illness Frodo comes to accept his wish to return to normality is impossible and embraces instead Arwen's great gift (*Letters* 329). In an earlier draft of the tale, he explicitly wishes to leave before he is ill again (*Sauron Defeated* 112).

After Bag End becomes again habitable, Frodo asks Sam what time he will come to live with him. The gardener presents his heart to his master. He wishes to remain with him, but he also desires to marry Rosie Cotton. The Ring-bearer handily solves this dilemma by welcoming them both into his home after their wedding. Despite all Frodo's pain, he considers himself one fortunate hobbit. In his dark days, he can bask in the light of his guardian's nurturing love and know, broken as he is, his Sam still cherishes him. He is never without the gem Arwen gave him and many times draws upon it for comfort.

As the year passes, Frodo withdraws completely from Shire society. Sinclair notes, "The emotional pain of PTSD engrosses the victim to such a degree that there is neither energy nor reason to reach out beyond the self; the inner warfare is profound and consumes from within" (68-69).

Criteria D of PTS is associated with "Inability to remember an important aspect of the traumatic event(s) (typically due to dissociative amnesia . . .). . . . Negative alterations in cognitions and mood associated with traumatic event(s), beginning or worsening after the traumatic event(s) occurred. . . . Persistent and exaggerated negative beliefs or expectations about oneself. . . . Persistent, distorted cognitions about the cause or consequences of the traumatic event(s) that lead the individual to blame himself/herself or others. . . . Persistent negative emotional state (e.g. fear, horror, anger, guilt, or shame) . . . [and] Markedly diminished interest or participation in significant activities" (*DSM* 271, 272).

Tolkien noted not only does Frodo carry the burden of "nightmare memories of past horrors . . . , but also unreasoning self-reproach: he saw himself and all that he done as a broken failure" (*Letters* 328). "It is possible that once the ring was destroyed he had little recollection of the last scene" (*Letters* 252). The Ring-bearer relies on Sam's memories. The gardener does not lie, but he remains innocent enough and not harmed enough to fully comprehend the terribleness of the Ring's violation of his master. Frodo needs time and distance, as well as grace, wisdom, and the counsel of others to fully comprehend the enormity himself. Based on what Sam said he heard him say, the Ring-bearer believes he made a free choice to claim it. The gardener noted Frodo used a tone of voice he never used before, which gives another sign it was not truly his own will.

But Frodo would not consider this of any consequence. The words themselves indict him - or seem to. He would hear "*I* do not choose to do . . . *I* will not do . . . The Ring is *mine*" echo in untrue emphasis and believe he spoke them. Who else could have? Though not in reference to the Ring-bearer, the words of Kurt Brunner and Jim Ware still apply: "We are ruled by what we believe, whether it's true or not" (102). Because the hobbit judges he made a conscious and consented choice, he assigns to himself greater blame and responsibility than was truly there. A person's idea an evil act was actively willed by them "may be the most devastating of all guilt-producing thoughts because it makes you doubt your own goodness as a human being" (Goulston 150).

Just as the story of the Quest quickly became distorted and larger than life as Ioreth told it, the sense of failure grow in Frodo's mind. In this state of guilt and shame, and fully aware lust for the Ring continues to burn him, he does not understand the truth yet. With all the other memories stolen from him, he seems to forget what he learned after Weathertop. He realized then what appeared his own desire to put on the Ring was actually the press of the Ringwraiths' combined wills until he crumbled under the assault. He also forgets what he told Sam in Mordor about his awareness he was nearly in the Ring's power. In order to heal, he needs to remember and understand "I do not choose" means literally that. Until then, self-loathing would continue to overwhelm him. John Garth notes Frodo's state of mind echoes in the book, *George Sherston*, written by WWI veteran, Siegfried Sassoon, as a thinly veiled autobiography:

. . . inwardly I was restless and overwrought. My war had stopped, but its after-effects were still with me. I couldn't sleep . . . my thoughts couldn't escape themselves into that completed peace which was the only thing I wanted. I saw myself as one who had achieved nothing except an idiotic anti-climax, and my mind worked itself into a tantrum of self-disparagement. (qtd. in "Frodo" 52)

Charles Moorman remarks, "The tragic events of the struggle against evil are seen throughout *The Lord of the Rings*, particularly in Frodo. . . until, almost like Gollum, he becomes 'enslaved to that Ring, unable to find peace or relief ever in life again'" (65). Susan Ang understands both the truth and Frodo's take on it:

The loss of Frodo's finger . . . is a complex and powerful image. . . . It speaks of loss and pain, but also a muted triumph. It is a sign of the hero who had endured. . . . It is, however, also a sign of flaw, the absent finger an ever-present reminder of inadequacy and failure, of inability at the last moment to yield up the Ring to the fire. Neither idea - 'Frodo as hero' or 'Frodo as failure' - has more weight than the other (80).

But for Frodo, the weight of inadequacy and failure crushes him. Flieger notes this "deeper, self-inflicted" injury is the hobbit's "greatest unhealed wound" ("Body" 291). The truth he was indeed a hero and not a failure at all has no substance for him. Ang continues, "That inadequacy and incompleteness is, however, capable of redemption. This is perhaps nowhere more powerfully pointed out than in the fact that the 'redemption' - or saving - of Frodo and the completion of the quest take place at the hands of one himself inadequate and incomplete, unwilling and unaware" (81). One can hope Frodo learned to see the loss of his finger as a sign of mercy. He could have lost so much more.

Sam's heart aches the Shire hobbits do not care or understand what his master did out of love for them and all Middle-earth. Frodo sacrificed everything in a silent martyrdom no unharmed hobbit can comprehend. Merry, Pippin, and Sam received some glimpses of torment through the Black Breath, looking into the *palantír*, and carrying the Ring. They could relate a little. Still no one endured what Frodo had; none were so violently raped until his entire identity was in shreds.

Frodo does not know how to fill the gaping hole where his identity once was. The Quest consumed every shred of strength and self he had. He is neither any longer an innocent, carefree hobbit, nor is he a Ring-bearer for the Ring is no more. His present is empty. He is a shell.

The following October, Sam discovers Frodo in the throes of another flashback and hears him speak of unrecoverable injuries. This time the illness "seemed to pass and he was quite himself the next day" (*LotR* VI:9, 1002). The first two illnesses clearly state recovery takes place, but as this one only "seemed" over, recovery is incomplete at best. Perhaps it heralds a sign Frodo is more aware of his lost time and so better at concealing from Sam how ill he really is. It would also make clear to himself how he struggles with his 'new normal' way of life. Each new illness gives Saruman's foretelling of a short and unhealthy life fresh opportunity to sink tougher roots in Frodo's heart.

The next March Frodo puts forth a fully conscious attempt to hide his fourth illness from Sam. There is no mention at all of a recovery, whether in seeming or truth. The first of the Gamgee brood makes her appearance a fortnight later. Elanor is but one of the manifold blessings from the sacrifices her father and Frodo made two years previously. She will not long know the master of Bag End. His way West is long decided and almost upon him. Trudy G. Shaw offers another meditation on Frodo's dark night of the soul:

> In his suffering - both physical and otherwise - after he returns to the Shire, he is facing a darkness he has no control over, although he can always decide how to respond to it. John of the Cross saw the passive night of the spirit as the most intense of the nights, when every spiritual light a

person has traveled by is blown out. . . . that's the person's perception. The reality is that the light of God is so close (or, perhaps better, the person has become so open to it) that the person is blinded by it, but what's *experienced* is complete spiritual darkness. Passing through this night requires the person to continue on the Road guided by nothing but faith. We know that Frodo has continued his journey *because* he sails West; otherwise, he wouldn't have accepted the invitation. Even so, he doesn't seem to see his leaving Middle-earth as a way out of his suffering. He tells Sam that he has been "too deeply hurt" to take up his old life in the Shire, but in the scenes leading up to his embarkation he doesn't mention any hope of healing. He leaves Middle-earth for the same reason that he originally left Bag End and then Rivendell: he's been called, and he responds as he always has, with each response requiring more faith and trust than the one before it. ("dark and empty"; emphasis in original)

Frodo completes his part of the memoirs of the War of the Ring. It falls to Sam to finish it. Stephen C. Winter notes:

Frodo displays his wisdom once again in leaving the empty pages. He knows that the story does not end with his departure from it. . . .

Frodo knows that wisdom is, at least in part, a knowing that we are smaller than the big story but his book, in itself a continuation of something that Bilbo began, displays another wisdom too. He displays it in the title that he chooses . . .

Frodo has seen the great events of his time in a way that no-one else can. It is the perspective of "the Little People". When hobbits come to read his story they are meant to understand that in the eyes of the world they are small but they are meant to understand their greatness too. ("Frodo Finishes")

The Ring-bearer leaves moving testimony within the Red Book of his physical trials. He remains almost silent about his worst pain. Or does he? Sam told his master more than once on the Quest not to speak of traumatic events. The remarkable poem, "The Sea-Bell," provides evidence he may have, if viewed through the lens of its subtitle, *Frodos Dreme*. Tolkien wrote the Ring-bearer was probably not the scribe of the piece himself, but notes one can observe within it the "dark and despairing dreams which visited him in March and October during his last three years" ("Adventures" [ATB] 9). Given the hobbit's propensity to talk in his sleep, as Gandalf noted in Rivendell, Sam could have recorded the poem from the Ring-bearer's own lips. Certainly the words haunted the unknown recorder enough to associate it with him.

If the traveler in the poem and Frodo are one and the same, it gives heart-wrenching evidence of the depth of damage done to the Ring-bearer. The call of the sea-bell and the arrival of the ship appear invitations to journey to a far land. A ship is ready to take Frodo as well. The traveler's arrival at a distant shore begins pleasantly enough. He drinks to his heart's content and soaks in beautiful sights and songs. But it soon turns to a place of rejection and despair rather than welcome and hope. Any time the sojourner approaches those who sing, they disappear and the music ceases. No one speaks to him even after he pleads someone do so. Frodo knew of the flight of the Mirkwood Elves from Bilbo and the dwarves. He faces his own shunning after he returns to the Shire. The traveler's self-proclamation as king to echoes the moment Frodo believes he freely claimed the Ring. The madness that falls upon the sojourner recalls the hobbit's memories of Gollum's wretchedness: "Like a dark mole groping I went, / to the ground falling, on my hands crawling . . ." (ATB 59).

The traveler, now more of a trespasser, remains in this pitiful state for a little over a year. In winter, the boat returns him to where he came from. But there is still no welcome for him. He talks only to himself because those he encounters ignore him. Flieger observes, "He is changed forever, taken out of his time, lost from the otherworld and estranged from his own, very much as Frodo was after his return from Mordor to the Shire, not just 'falling asleep again' but caught in a nightmare from which he cannot waken" (*Question* 216).

Peacefulness is not Frodo's to find any longer in Middle-earth. Gandalf's words about incurable wounds carry increasing weight, as the hobbit endures the daily struggle to live in a world and within a shattered self that without the Ring is "dark and empty" (*LotR* VI:9,1001). His guilt and sense of failure make him especially vulnerable to the fear peace will be unavailable anywhere. "If the speaker is Frodo, the reader is being told that he sees himself as irrecoverably lost, condemned to a half life that is no life at all, suspended between two worlds. His sacrifice has led to no redemption. Something in Tolkien wanted the reader to hear Frodo in the poem and to link the poem's situation with what might have happened to him" (Flieger, *Splintered* 163). Tom Shippey notes that subtitle of the poem points in part to "a sense of ultimate defeat and loss in the hero of *The Lord of the Rings*. Frodo doubted his own salvation" (*Road* 285).

"I must find the sea! / I have lost myself, and I know not the way, / but let me gone!" (ATB 59). Though the traveler speaks these words after he loses his trust of the land where he first found haven but then rejection, Flieger notes, "His despairing cry . . . recalls Frodo at the end of *The Lord of the Rings*" (*Splintered* 162).

The light that comes to the traveler after a lengthy darkness means leaving the place which broke him. For Frodo, the possibility of the journey West remains before him and illuminates the dark places of his anguish. The traveler throws away everything he has. He loses the awe of the far shore, at first so marvelous, but now such a wasteland with no solace or peace. The loss of awe is "the inability to believe that there can be anything greater than that which inflicted the original pain. . . . All has been rendered insignificant by the awfulness of the trauma" (Sinclair 72). How frightening the agony of Frodo's splintered heart and spirit is stronger than the powerful presence of his friends' love for him. Christine Chism notes the empty shell cast away "is what Frodo in his darkest moments feels he has become" (71). Flieger observes:

Whoever the voice in 'The Sea-bell' is intended to be . . . the words of the poem, the suffering of the speaker, describe an experience all too recognizable to anyone who lived through it, of alienation from the reference points of familiar experience, of a world gone past the point of no return, longing for something it once had and ought to have been able to keep. (*Question* 224)

[T]he speaker in 'The Sea-bell' (who may be Frodo, is certainly Tolkien, and very probably all humanity) is important to the myth precisely because he experiences change. He is a man of antitheses, both spiritually and literally between worlds, having lost one and not yet gained another. He is poised in the moment of greatest loss, which paradoxically will bring with it the experience of becoming. (*Splintered* 171)

Flieger notes the poem is of "such unmitigated alienation and despair as to negate hope of any kind" (*Splintered* 162). But she adds, "[T]he 'dreme' (if it is a dream) should be seen over against another dream which gives a considerably more hopeful . . . picture. This is Frodo's last dream in the house of Tom Bombadil" (*Splintered* 164), which gives the Ring-bearer a vision of his future home in the West.

To Be Re-made

Frodo's path went East before it could come West. In earlier drafts of the story, Tolkien already foresaw the hobbit would go to the Undying Lands, long before either knew of the deep wounds which would drive the Ring-bearer there (*Shadow* 380). Only because he forsook the light and endured the darkness of his Road did he receive the tremendous boon to come back to the light. He makes this choice within the grip of a torment he has no hope to ease while inside the confines of the mortal world. The sacrifices he made in body, mind, heart, and soul are so complete what remains is not enough to sustain him in Middle-earth.

During the Quest, Sam taught Frodo about the radical hope which refused to give up no matter how full of despair things appeared. The Ring-bearer's dreams may reflect the fear the blessing to come West is false, and as the traveler in the poem found, he will reach for it and find it empty and himself even more desolate and alone. His courage to make the decision to leave nonetheless demonstrates he does not allow this to overwhelm him. Inspired by Sam, some hope still struggles to live amid the ruins in the dark world Frodo finds himself in. It gives him the strength to believe he will not be forsaken by all but welcomed as a guest. He casts away the empty shell of his life in Middle-earth and readies himself to embrace the possibility of becoming filled again. In this hope, or the desperation of the traveler, or both, he chooses to flee. He takes the chance his fears are not reality and instead healing and peace await him. It will take hard work to redefine himself and allow light and joy to enter his world again and to embrace a self who does not forget the black night but is no longer ruled by it. But at last, he would no longer be trapped in the Sammath Naur at the moment of his greatest violation and loss. He could descend the Mountain and let go of the crushing burden of guilt and failure.

Almost on the anniversary of his first Quest, Frodo begins this journey. On his birthday, he and Sam come to where they hid from the Ringwraith. The gardener listens as his master sings his own version of Bilbo's walking song. Judith Klinger remarks, "This verse implies Frodo's ability to discover 'hidden paths' that lead beyond the dimension of the mortal world . . ." ("Hidden Paths" 200). Though the Ring-bearer did not trod upon the pathways to the Havens before, he uses them now, as will Sam one day. William Reynolds also notes the changes Frodo makes to the song:

> . . . Frodo's last poem and the Elves' response are of vital importance since they establish that Bilbo's lighted inn symbol does not merely stand for a sense of satisfaction at following a hard task through to the end but for a different sort of life beyond that of the Road. While walking near the spot where he had first encountered the Black Rider, Frodo recites his last poem, a revision of the walking song he had sung after that meeting nearly three years before. The choice is a good one, for it transfers the trust and confidence with which Frodo began his first, and ultimately successful, journey to his second trip and suggests that now as then his faith is well-placed.
>
> The suggestion is carried further by Frodo's awareness that what is happening is but another stage in the larger plan. (15)

In another echo of the Quest, the hobbits hear Elven voices call upon Elbereth and wait to meet them. Just as before, Gildor and his company come, but this time with Bilbo, Elrond, and Galadriel. The ancient hobbit greets Frodo and asks if he plans to accompany him on the next grand adventure. The Ring-bearer replies he does.

Frodo movingly tells Sam of his hope to restart his peaceful life in the Shire, only to watch this dream turn to dust. Peter S. Beagle notes:

> *The Lord of the Rings* is the tale of Frodo's journey through a long nightmare of greed and terrible energy, of his education in both fear and true beauty, and of his final loss of the world he seeks to save. In a sense, his growing knowledge has eaten up the joy and the innocent strength that made him, of all the wise and magic people he encounters, the only

one fit to bear the Ring. As he tells Sam . . . , 'It must often be so . . . when things are in danger: someone has to give them up, lose them, so that others may keep them.' There are others in Middle-earth who would have willingly paid that price, but certainly none to whom it would have meant as much. (xi)

Frodo surrenders his beloved homeland and leaves it in Sam's more than capable hands. "True courage is not so much about self-glorification as it is about self-emptying: being willing to be the bridge over which others may cross to safety" (Markos 68). Tom Shippey notes Frodo's sacrifice here echoes in

the words on the [WWI] Imphal-Kohima monument, now itself largely forgotten . . . .

'When you go home tell them of us and say
For your tomorrow we gave our today.' (*Author* 156)

Frodo's second sight reveals itself once more in astonishingly accurate predictions of Sam's future as Mayor and patriarch of a large family. The Ring-bearer specifically names several of the Gamgee children with the acknowledgement even more may come. Hannah Eagleson observes how well these fit Sam:

It takes into account his natural interests and the ones he learned growing up, such as gardening. It recognizes things Sam has always cared about but that people haven't always seen in him, such as his interest in storytelling. [It] . . . also acknowledges the growth in skill and character that Sam has achieved on the journey, which will allow him to do things he could not have before, such as become mayor. And it places the skills and growth Sam has learned on his exciting travels in the context of the home Sam has always loved, the Shire. (*Wisdom: ROTK* 66)

This last sacrifice Frodo makes is no easier than any of the others. "Frodo's choice to leave is an act of utter humility and self-denial" (Driggers 149). Though it breaks the hearts of the Ring-bearer and his faithful companion (with Frodo's broken long before), both come to see this as a gift, at once terrible and wondrous. Terrible in its sad necessity, but also in the other sense of the word: what an astoundingly powerful grace for Frodo to receive. The three hobbits become "filled with a sadness that was yet blessed and without bitterness . . ." (*LotR* VI:9, 1006).

The Red Book holds no record Bilbo or Frodo spoke further on the way to the Havens. Perhaps what they experience, especially the younger Baggins, would be too profound or painful for words. They say goodbye to the Shire and their entire way of life in Middle-earth. For Bilbo, this would be easier because he is so much older and near the end of his life and has not lived in the Shire for 20 years. For Frodo, this long goodbye to things he would never see, hear, touch, or smell again is necessary. "Some readers have said that by the end of *LotR*, Frodo and Bilbo have become more similar to elves than to hobbits, and in some aspects that may be true. But in some ways, perhaps they've become the highest expression of hobbit simplicity, nonpossessiveness, and lack of desire for power" (Shaw, "Ring"). The Ring was the reason they had to part in Rivendell for the Quest. It also brings them back together at the end.

Even as far back as the Golden Wood, an admirer believes Frodo made this choice:

> Why is it perilous to enter [Lórien]?
>
> Perhaps because entering the otherworld forces a choice on the traveller - a choice between worlds, between perceptions, different existences. Frodo does make a choice, in the end - he chooses to 'trade' his 'reality' for that of the Elves . . . .
>
> . . .
>
> . . . One can almost imagine Frodo & Sam standing on ships, anchored side by side, holding hands, but their ships are facing in different directions, & when the anchors are

raised, they will slowly lose their grip & pass away in different directions.

We see in them different choices, freely made. Their love holding them together, but their choices pulling them apart.

. . . [Frodo] is who he is, & his choice is a spiritual one, reflecting, ultimately, his essential nature. . . . Frodo is as 'half-Elven' as a mortal can be. . . . (davem)

Gandalf and Círdan greet the company as they arrive at the Grey Havens. Alison Milbank beautifully and profoundly describes the enduring bond Frodo shares with his Sam and their physical sundering here:

The main problem for the reader is how to separate in his or her mind two characters who have been a pair all through the novel, and who belong together. Despite his marriage, parenthood and obvious delight in Shire life, Sam is incomplete without Frodo, and Frodo an attenuated presence without Sam's earthliness. . . . For Frodo hardly seems to have a body at all in the later parts of *The Lord of the Rings,* and even his pains back home in the Shire have a spiritual basis. Sam, on the contrary, is not just a reassuring physical presence but an active agent in the rebuilding of his community, and in forming human relationships. The true happy ending of the novel lies beyond the pages of the book, and yet is anticipated in moments such as Sam and Frodo's descent from Mount Doom, when Sam, a true Bunyanesque 'Hopeful', leads the lost and broken Frodo to safety, just as he had borne Frodo and the Ring up to the summit, and found the burden surprisingly light. Sam is not to be reduced to an allegory of the body, for he is much more than that, but the separation of the two at the Grey Havens is emblematic of the sorrow of the separation of the soul and body at death, while their solidarity gives a taste of the ecstatic reunion of soul and body at the Resurrection. (111)

Frodo is "committed to water . . . to be healed of his wounds" (Flieger, "Body" 157). As the ship departs, he holds up Galadriel's phial for his friends to watch until both ship and light disappear from their sight. "A final glimmer emanates from the crystal decanter: the light of Eärendil - a symbol of enduring hope, determination and wisdom that will never fade" (Smith 188). The Ring-bearer's precognitive dream in Tom's house comes true. Flieger notes, "[T]he reader and Frodo have suffered through so much together that [the Undying Lands] first appearance now seems to have been not occult but heaven-sent, an epiphany, a promise of the best that could happen - the antidote, if we had but known it, to all that was yet to come" (*Question* 189).

"Frodo's journey, a voyage of the soul as well as of the body, is continuing, and its final end is not revealed to the reader" (Flieger, *Interrupted* 79). Even though we do not know for certain it ends on a happy note, Judith Klinger speaks for all who hope for this:

> There may be no guarantees [your time *may* come, not it *would* come] but the remaining hope is not . . . a vague, universal hope that all mortals share. It is, quite specifically, tied to Sam's wish at Cirith Ungol and his ability to reinterpret ultimate separation as a hope for reunion. At the very last, we are reminded that Sam's apparently impossible 'one wish' did come true. ("Hidden Paths" 207; emphasis in original)

Sam saw in the terrible darkness of Shelob's Lair death was not a permanent end to his relationship with his beloved master. Rather it was a door through which it could continue. Surely his heart hopes the vast gulf of the Sea is no barrier either. The powerful bond between their hearts and souls transcends all physical distances. While the gardener's body stands on the shore, his heart travels with his beloved master. He sees what Frodo sees and assures himself of his master's safe arrival.

At the very end of the text, Frodo's . . . dream-vision stands out as the ultimate 'realization of imagined wonder', a capacity attributed to Sam from the very beginning of the book. The journey to Eressëa, as envisioned by Sam, exemplifies not only the convergence of history and myth but a state of altered consciousness; it is at once real and imagined and blends visionary experience with an actual entry into Faërie. This conclusive moment of crossing the threshold into Other Time is Sam's contribution to the Tale and could not have been achieved by any other author or participant in the events. (Klinger, "Strange Powers" 90-91)

"Sam's day is ending; he is going back into that same Shire that has been night and dream for Frodo. Frodo's night is over, and his sunrise brings daylight and waking, a real awakening this time, in which what was dream is now the true reality" (Flieger, *Question* 205).

Linda Greenwood speaks movingly of Frodo's time in the West:

As part of her sacrifice, as part of her choice of the gift of death, Arwen gives Frodo the passage into the West that she has forsaken for mortality on Middle-earth. . . . Frodo goes off to a kind of Otherworld where dwell the immortal. He is not, however, going to his true resting place. His future is still cloaked in mystery, and although he has hope, it is hope deferred. The land he sets out for is a place he cannot truly belong to or rest in: a place he cannot truly go to. Derrida speaks of the same journey: 'It is only when you give yourself to, surrender to, and set out for the wholly other, for the impossible, only when you go where you cannot go that you are really on the move' (qtd. in Caputo 50). The search for the 'wholly other,' for God, can never be fully realized on earth. That is the point of faith. It is a faith in the hope of glory, a glory that gives glimpses but can only give them in passing, a glory that can be seen not yet face to face but only in a mirror darkly. This faith does not stay in one place, but keeps moving and growing, spurred on by the power of love, a love that realizes that perfection cannot be realized here on earth, but resides in a dimension not discernible to the human eye. (192-193)

Frodo's sojourn in the Blessed Realm would be a time of purification, rest, enlightenment, and healing; a time to feel joy and peace again; to be cured of the lingering guilt, shame, and desire for the Ring; to have his soul healed of the many fiery darts of the Enemy; to understand he was only a small mortal with an imperfect, fallible strength and will, but also the great hero Elrond foresaw.

Ilúvatar waited long to bring His beloved child to this point. As a being who came from outside Middle-earth inflicted the damage done to the Ring-bearer's heart and soul, the cure, if it could be found, had to also come from outside it. Only Ilúvatar Himself could have borne Frodo's crushing burden without breaking. Only He and the Valar can heal him of the wounds from the heavy cross He received permission to place on such small shoulders. During the excruciating birthing process to become who the hobbit was meant, he died to who he previously defined himself as. Here in the West, he has the chance to rise from the ashes stronger. Hopefully through peaceful reflection, he learns he was emptied for a purpose: so he could be filled again. The great boon initiated through Arwen's request provides him a means to fully discover he was not only the beloved child of Primula and Drogo, but also of his Creator, and why out of all people the One chose him

Filled once more, Frodo would not remain lost in darkness. He would live fully again and in the Light. In the end, he would become what Gandalf foresaw in Rivendell. Would he shine so brightly if not burnished by the crucible of the Quest? What a wonder Sam must have beheld!

Through an analogy from St. Thérèse, the Little Flower, Trudy G. Shaw gives a loving tribute to Frodo's faith in the unseen, unknown One who chose him:

> Think of yourself as a small child, Thérèse said, who wants to climb a staircase because you know your Father is at the top and you want to go to him. You . . . lift your little foot, but your legs are too short to reach the next step. . . .

Meanwhile, your Father sees you. . . . His heart fills with love and pity for you, and he . . . picks you up and carries you in his arms to the top. 'But,' she added, 'we have to keep lifting our little foot.'

. . .

. . . Frodo kept lifting his foot, too, both figuratively and literally. The fact that he kept doing so didn't make it possible for him to save Middle-earth, or himself. But it came from his desire to save Middle-earth. . . . For both Thérèse and Frodo, it came from love. . . . And, although the child doesn't climb the stairs and Frodo doesn't save Middle-earth, the stairs *are* climbed and Middle-earth *is* saved. ("Thérèse"; emphasis in original)

Tolkien noted for mortals allowed access to the Undying Lands, this gave them "[a]n opportunity for dying according to the original plan for the unfallen: they went to a state in which they could acquire greater knowledge and peace of mind, and being healed of all hurts both of mind and body, could at last surrender themselves: die of free will, and even of desire, in *estel*" (*Morgoth's Ring* 341). "Frodo Baggins allows himself to be transplanted that the tree of his life not die completely, and it is to be hoped that he regains his strength and beauty again before he is ready for the final harvest and is gathered at last into the Creator's storehouse" (Larner).

But the souls of the virtuous are
in the hands of God . . .
In the eyes of the unwise,
they did appear to die,
their going looked like a disaster,
their leaving us, like annihilation;
but they are in peace. . . .
God has put them to the test
and proved them worthy to be with him;
he has tested them like gold in a furnace,
and accepted them as a holocaust.
When the time comes for his visitation,
they will shine out. . . . (Wis. 3:1-3, 5-7a)

Bibliography

Agan, Cami. "Song as Mythic Conduit in *The Fellowship of the Ring*." *Mythlore*, vol. 26, no. 3/4, issue 101/102, 2008, 41-63.

Ang, Susan. *Master of the Rings: Inside the World of J. R. R. Tolkien*. Totem Books, 2002.

Arthur, Sarah. *Walking with Bilbo*. Tyndale, 2005.

Baillie, C. "Frodo and Grace." *Christianity and Middle-earth*, en-tropyhouse.com/baillie/candme/essays/frodo-andgrace.html. Accessed 13 Aug 2018.

Bassham, Gregory. "The Adventurous Hobbit." Bassham and Bronson, 7-19.

Bassham, Gregory, and Eric Bronson, editors. The Hobbit *and Philosophy*. John Wiley & Sons, 2012.

Beagle, Peter S. "My Boy Gollum." Forward. *More People's Guide to J. R. R. Tolkien*, by Cliff Broadway, et al. Cold Spring Press, 2005, 11-15.

Bell, James Stuart. *The Spiritual World of* The Hobbit. Bethany House, 2013.

Benedict XVI. *Jesus of Nazareth: From the Baptism in the Jordan to the Transfiguration*. Translated by Adrian J. Walker, Doubleday, 2007

Bradley, Marion Zimmer. "Men, Halflings, and Hero-Worship." Isaacs and Zimbardo, *Tolkien and the Critics*, 109-127.

Bonhoeffer, Dietrich. *The Cost of Discipleship*. Macmillan, 1959.

---. *Letters and Papers From Prison*. Fortress Press, 2015.

Brown, Devin. *The Christian World of* The Hobbit. Abingdon, 2012.

Bruner, Kurt, and Jim Ware. *Finding God in* The Lord of the Rings. Tyndale, 2001.

Caldecott, Stratford. *The Power of the Ring*. Rev. ed., Crossroad, 2012.

Chance, Jane. *Tolkien's Art: A Mythology for England*. Rev ed., The UP of Kentucky, 2001.

Child of the 7th Age. "The Barrow-downs Discussion Forums > Middle-earth > The Books > Chapter-by-Chapter – LotR - Book 1 - Chapter 01 - A Long-Expected Party." *The Barrow-*

Downs,   23   Jun   2004,   forum.barrow-
downs.com/showthread.php?t=10833. Accessed 28 May
2018.

Christensen, Bonniejean. "Gollum's Character Transformation in
The Hobbit." *A Tolkien Compass.* Edited by Jared Lobdell,
Open Court, 1975, 9-28.

Chism, Christine. "Middle-earth, the Middle Ages, and the Aryan
nation: Myth and history in World War II." *Tolkien the Medi-
evalist.* Edited by Jane Chance, Routledge, 2003, 63-92.

Crowe, Edith. "The Many Faces of Heroism in Tolkien." *Mythlore,*
vol. 10, no. 2, issue 36, 1983, 5-8.

Croft, Janet Brennan. *War and the Works of J. R. R. Tolkien.* Praeger,
2004.

davem. "The Barrow-downs Discussion Forums > Middle-earth >
The Books > Chapter-by-Chapter – LotR - Book 2 -
Chapter 06 - Lothórien." *The Barrow-Downs,* 22 Oct. 2004,
forum.barrowdowns.com/showthread.php?t=11274.
Accessed 16 Sept. 2018.

Dearborn, Kerry. "The Sacrament of the Stranger in C. S. Lewis, J.
R. R. Tolkien, and George MacDonald." *Truths Breathed
Through Silver: The Inklings' Moral and Mythopoeic Legacy.* Edited
by Jonathan B. Himes et al., Cambridge Scholars Publishing,
2008, 138-150.

Delsigne, Jill. "Hobbits, Tolkien and God: Writing Eucatastrophe
and the Problem of Evil." Wells, II:99-107.

Diagnostic and Statistical Manual of Mental Disorders. 5th edition,
American Psychiatric Association, 2013.

Dreamflower. "Dreamflower's Musings: The Importance of Being
Bilbo."   *Stories   of   Arda,*
storiesofarda.com/chapterview.asp?sid=4201&cid=23156.
Accessed 16 Sept. 2018.

Driggers, Taylor. "Modern Medievalism and Myth: Tolkien,
Tennyson and the Quest for a Hero." *Journal   of   Inkling
Studies,* vol. 3, no. 2, 2013, 133-152.

Eagleson, Hannah. *Walking to Wisdom: Teachers Edition: The Fellowship
of the Ring.* Classical Academic Press, 2014.

---. *Walking to Wisdom: Teachers Edition: The Two Towers.* Classical Academic Press, 2014.

---. *Walking to Wisdom: Teachers Edition: The Return of the King.* Classical Academic Press, 2014.

Ellen Virginia. "When I am Weak, Then I Am Strong: Frodo's Providential Heroism." *Fellowship and Fairydust,* 29 Aug. 2017, fellowshipandfairydust.com/2017/08/29/when-i-am-weak-i-am-strong/. Accessed 16 Sept. 2018.

Frailey, A. K. *The Road Goes Ever On: A Christian Journey Through* The Lord of the Rings. iUniverse, 2011.

Finch, Thomas. *Unmapped Darkness: Finding God's Path Through Suffering.* Moody, 2006.

Flieger, Verlyn. *A Question of Time: J. R. R. Tolkien's Road to Faërie.* Kent State UP, 1997.

---. *Interrupted Music: The Making of Tolkien's Mythology.* Kent State UP, 2005.

---. *Splintered Light: Logos and Language in Tolkien's World.* Rev. ed., Kent State UP, 2002.

---. "The Body in Question: The Unhealed Wounds of Frodo Baggins." *Green Suns and Faërie: Essays on J. R. R. Tolkien.* Kent State UP, 2012, 283-291.

---. "Missing Person." *Green Suns and Faërie,* 223-231.

---. "The Music and the Task: Fate and Free Will in Middle-earth." *Green Suns and Faërie.* 14-40.

Frankl, Viktor E. *Man's Search for Meaning.* Beacon Press, 2006.

Franklin, Jentezen. *Believe That You Can.* Charisma House, 2008.

Fuller, Edmund. "The Lord of the Hobbits: J. R. R. Tolkien." Isaacs and Zimbardo, *Tolkien and the Critics,* 17-39.

Gardner, Patrick, et al. *SparkNotes: The Lord of the Rings.* Spark Publishing, 2002.

Gardner, Patrick, and Brian Phillips. *SparkNotes:* The Hobbit. Spark Publishing, 2002.

Garth, John. "Frodo and the Great War." The Lord of the Rings: *1954-2004: Scholarship in Honor of Richard E. Blackwelder.* Edited by Wayne G. Hammond and Christina Scull, Marquette UP, 2003, 41-56.

Goulston, Mark. *Post-Traumatic Stress Disorder for Dummies*. Wiley, 2007.

Gordon, Barry. "Kingship, Priesthood and Prophecy in *The Lord of the Rings*." *Cultural Collections, UON Library,* 13 May 2009, uoncc.wordpress.com/2009/05/13/kingship-priesthood-and-prophecy-in-the-lord-of-the-rings/. Accessed August 13, 2018.

Grant, Patrick. "Tolkien: Archetype and Word." Issacs and Zimbardo, *Understanding* The Lord of the Rings, 163-182.

Greenwood, Linda. "Love: 'The Gift of Death'." *Tolkien Studies, Volume II*, 2005, 171-195.

Gunton, Colin. "A Far-Off Gleam of the Gospel: Salvation in Tolkien's *The Lord of the Rings*." *Tolkien: A Celebration*. Edited by Joseph Pearce, Ignatius, 2001, 124-140.

Hallam, Andrew. "Thresholds to Middle-earth: Allegories of Reading, Allegories for Knowledge and Transformation." *Mythlore*, vol. 30, no 1/2, issue 115/116, 2011, 23-42.

Hammond, Wayne G., and Christina Scull. The Lord of the Rings: *A Reader's Companion*. Houghton Mifflin, 2005.

Hein, Ronald. *Christian Mythmakers*. 2nd. ed., Cornerstone, 2002.

Hillman, Tom. "Boromir, Fear, and the Pity of Frodo," *Alas, not me*, 17 Feb. 2016, alasnotme.blogspot.com/2016/02/boromir-fear-and-pity-of-frodo-fr-2x396.html. Accessed 2 Jun 2018.

---."Gollum's Blighted Repentance and What Bilbo Saw," *Alas, not me,* 18 Jan. 2015, alasnotme.blogspot.com/2015/01/gollums-blighted-repentance-and-what.html. Accessed 4 Jun 2018.

Hollingshead, Dan. "Frodo Walking Under Starlight." *Silver Leaves . . . from the White Tree of Hope*, issue 5, 2014, 60-61.

Ilverai. "Eucatastrophe, Discatastrophe and the destruction of the Ring." *Wandering Paths*, 10 Nov. 2012, ilverai.wordpress.com/2012/11/10/eucatastrophe-discatastrophe-and-the-destruction-of-the-ring/. Accessed 28 May 2018.

Isaacs, Neil D., and Rose A. Zimbardo, editors. *Tolkien and the Critics*. University of Notre Dame Press, 1968.

---. *Understanding* The Lord of the Rings. Houghton Mifflin Harcourt, 2005.

The Jerusalem Bible Reader's Edition. Edited by Alexander Jones, Doubleday, 1968.

Kilby, Clyde S. "Mythic and Christian Elements in Tolkien." *Myth, Allegory and Gospel: An Interpretation of J. R. R. Tolkien/C. S. Lewis/G. K. Chesterton/Charles Williams.* Edited by John Warwick Montgomery, Bethany Fellowship, 1974, 119-143.

Klinger, Judith. "The Fallacies of Power: Frodo's Resistance to the Ring." Wells, I:354-368.

---. "Hidden Paths of Time: March 13th and the Riddles of Shelob's Lair." *Tolkien and Modernity 2.* Edited by Thomas Honegger and Frank Weinreich, Walking Tree, 2006, 143-209.

---. "Tolkien's 'Strange Powers of the Mind': Dreams, Visionary History and Authorship." Klinger, *Sub-creating Middle-earth: Constructions of Authorship and the Works of J. R. R. Tolkien,* Walking Tree, 2012, 43-106.

Kocher, Paul H. *Master of Middle-earth: The Fiction of J. R. R. Tolkien.* Ballantine Books, 1977.

Kraus, Joe. "There and Back Again: A Song of Innocence and Experience." Bassham and Bronson, 234-249.

Larner. "Words of Explanation: Travellers in Four Elements." *Stories of Arda,* storiesofarda.com/chapterview.asp?sid=6539&cid=36267. Accessed 16 Sept. 2018.

Lewis, C. S. *The Four Loves.* Harcourt Brace Jovanovich, 1960.

---. *Mere Christianity.* HarperCollins, 2001.

Livingston, Michael. "The Shell-Shocked Hobbit: The First World War and Tolkien's Trauma of the Ring." *Mythlore,* vol. 25, no. 1/2, issue 95/96, 2006, 77-91.

Longenecker, Dwight. "Frodo and Thérèse: The Little Way Through Middle-earth." *National Catholic Register,* 5 Oct. 2013, www.ncregister.com/site/article/frodo-and-therese-the-little-way-through-middle-earth. Accessed 17 Sept. 2018.

Mark12_30. "The Barrow-downs Discussion Forums > Middle-earth > The Books > Chapter-by Chapter - LotR - Book 1

- Chapter 03 - Three is Company." *The Barrow-Downs*, 6 Jul 2004,forum.barrow-downs.com/showthread.php?s=621ce0fa6bc8fef8c05e223 24e0657b3&t=10866/. Accessed 29 May 2018.

Markos, Louis. *On the Shoulders of Hobbits: The Road to Virtue with Tolkien and Lewis*. Moody Publishers, 2012.

Marotta, Ray. "An Unexpected Hero." *Silver Leaves . . . from the White Tree of Hope*, issue 5, 2014, 73-77.

Martinez, Michael. "Beware that baker in the kitchen!" *Understanding Middle-earth*. ViviSphere, 2003, 423-431.

---. "What is the Significance of the White Stag in The Hobbit?" *Middle-earth and J. R. R. Tolkien Blog*, 4 Dec. 2012, middle-earth.xenite.org/what-is-the-significance-of-the-white-stag-in-the-hobbit/. Accessed 26 May 2018.

Mathews, Richard. *Lightning from a Clear Sky*. Borgo Press, 1978.

May, Gerald. *Addiction and Grace: Love and Spirituality in the Healing of Addictions*. HarperCollins, 1991.

Milbank, Alison. *Chesterton and Tolkien as Theologians: The Fantasy of the Real*. T&T Clark, 2008.

Mills, David. "The Writer of our Story: Divine Providence in *The Lord of the Rings*." *Touchstone*, January-February 2002, touchstonemag.com/archives/article.php?id=15-01-022-f. Accessed 28 May 2018.

Milos, Karen. "Too Deeply Hurt: Understanding Frodo's Decision to Depart." *Mallorn* 36, 1998, 17-23.

Mishra, Jigyasa. "Who do you think is the true hero of The Lord of the Rings. How is your choice different for the movies (if at all)." *Quora*, 15 Apr. 2018. www.quora.com/Who-do-you-think-is-the-true-hero-of-The-Lord-of-the-Rings-How-is-your-choice-different-for-the-movies-if-at-all. Accessed 14 Jun 2018.

Moorman, Charles. "'Now Entertain Conjecture of a Time' - The Fictive Worlds of C. S. Lewis and J. R. R. Tolkien." *Shadows of Imagination: The Fantasies of C. S. Lewis, J. R. R. Tolkien and Charles Williams*. New Edition. Edited by Mark R. Hillegas, Southern Illinois UP, 1979, 59-69.

Murnane, Ben. "Frodo's Band of Brothers: Myth, Morality, and Reality in J. R. R. Tolkien and Stephen Ambrose." *VII: An Anglo-American Literary Review*, vol. 29, 2012, 5-16.

O'Donohue, John. Prologue. *The Confession of Saint Patrick*. Translated by John Skinner, Image Books/Doubleday, 1998, vii-xvi.

O'Neill, Timothy R. *The Individuated Hobbit: Jung, Tolkien and the Archetypes of Middle-earth*. Houghton Mifflin, 1979.

Olsen, Corey. *Exploring J. R. R. Tolkien's* The Hobbit. Houghton Mifflin Harcourt, 2012.

Palmer, Bruce. *Of Orc Rags, Phials & a Far Shore: Visions of Paradise in* The Lord of the Rings. Boar's Head, 1981.

Petty, Anne. *Tolkien in the Land of Heroes*. Cold Spring Press, 2003.

Pienciak, Anne M. *Barron's Book Notes: J. R. R. Tolkien's* The Hobbit *and* The Lord of the Rings. Barron's Educational Series, 1986.

Piosenniel. "The Barrows-Downs Discussion Forum > Middle-Earth Discussions > The Books > The Light in Frodo's Face." *The Barrow-Downs*, May 2, 2002, forum.barrow-downs.com/showthread.php?t=1318&highlight=light+frodo. Accessed 4 Jun 2018.

Purtill, Richard. *J. R. R. Tolkien: Myth, Morality, and Religion*. Ignatius, 2003.

Rapier, Douglas Charles. "Frodo's Temptation, Frodo's Failure." Wells, I:296-303.

Rateliff, John D. *The History of* The Hobbit *Part One: Mr. Baggins*. Houghton Mifflin Harcourt, 2007.

Reynolds, William. "Poetry as Metaphor in *The Lord of the Rings*." *Mythlore*, vol. 4, no. 4, issue 16, 1977, 12-16.

Rosebury, Brian. *Tolkien: A Cultural Phenomenon*. Palgrave Macmillan, 2003.

Rutledge, Fleming. *The Battle for Middle-earth: Tolkien's Divine Design in* The Lord of the Rings. Eerdmans, 2004.

Sale, Roger. "Tolkien and Frodo Baggins." Isaacs and Zimbardo, *Tolkien and the Critics*, 247-288.

Seeley, Andrew. "The Education of the Hobbits in *The Lord of the Rings*." *The Imaginative Conservative*, 29 Aug. 2014, www.theimaginativeconservative.org/2014/08/education-of-the-hobbits-in-the-lord-of-the-rings.html. Accessed 30 May 2018.

Shaw, Trudy G. "'all is dark and empty' Sixth mansions/The passive night of the spirit." *Frodo Lives...Within Us Now*, www.frodo-livesin.us/Catholicwork/id141.htm. Accessed 10 Jun 2018.

---. "'for I shall not be the same' transition from the fifth mansions to the passive night of the spirit." *Frodo Lives...Within Us Now*, www.frodolivesin.us/Catholicwork/id8.htm. Accessed 15 Jun 2018.

---."Frodo as Paradox." *Frodo Lives...Within Us Now*, www.frodo-livesin.us/Catholicwork/id86.htm. Accessed 3 Jun 2018.

---. "Gifted and Graced." *Frodo Lives...Within Us Now*, www.frodo-livesin.us/Catholicwork/id84.htm. Accessed 27 May 2018.

---. "'He lived alone...'" *Frodo Lives...Within Us Now*, www.frodo-livesin.us/Catholicwork/id121.htm. Accessed 27 May 2018.

---. "...in his dreams...?'" *Frodo Lives...Within Us Now*, www.frodo-livesin.us/Catholicwork/id108.htm. Accessed 29 May 2018.

---. "'I will take the Ring...' Fourth Mansions." *Frodo Lives...Within Us Now*, www.frodolivesin.us/Catholicwork/id139.htm. Accessed 3 Jun 2018.

---. "'naked in the dark' The active night of the spirit." *Frodo Lives...Within Us Now*, www.frodolivesin.us/Catholic-work/id65.htm. Accessed 9 Jun 2018.

---. "Thérèse and Frodo." *Frodo Lives...Within Us Now*, www.frodo-livesin.us/Catholicwork/id90.htm. Accessed 16 Sept. 2018.

---. "'They've taken everything' The passive night of the senses." *Frodo Lives...Within Us Now*, www.frodolivesin.us/Catholic-work/id64.htm. Accessed 8 Jun 2018.

---. "The Ring as Birthday Present." *Frodo Lives...Within Us Now*, www.frodolivesin.us/archives/id78.htm. Accessed 15 Jun 2018.

Shippey, Tom. *J. R. R. Tolkien: Author of the Century*. Houghton Mifflin, 2001.

---. *The Road to Middle-earth: How J. R. R. Tolkien Created a New Mythology*. Revised and expanded ed., Houghton Mifflin, 2003.

Shire Collective, The. *Unofficial Hobbit Handbook*. Writer's Digest Books, 2012.

Shmoop Editorial Team. "Fellowship of the Ring Friendship Quotes." *Shmoop*, 11 Nov. 2008, www.shmoop.com/fellowship-of-ring/friendship-quotes.html. Accessed 2 Jun 2018.

---."Sting in The Fellowship of the Ring." *Shmoop*, 11 Nov. 2008, www.shmoop.com/fellowship-of-ring/sting-symbol.html. Accessed 2 Jun 2018.

Sinclair, N. Duncan. *Horrific Traumata: A Pastoral Response to the Post-Traumatic Stress Disorder*. The Haworth Pastoral Press, 1993.

Sinex, Margaret. "'Tricksy Lights': Literary and Folkloric Elements in Tolkien's Passage of the Dead Marshes." *Tolkien Studies, Volume II*, 2005, 93-112.

Smith, Noble. *Wisdom of the Shire: A Short Guide to a Long and Happy Life*. St. Martin's Press, 2012.

Smol, Anna. "Frodo's Body: Liminality and the Experience of War." *The Body in Tolkien's Legendarium*. Edited by Christopher Vaccaro, McFarland, 2013, 39-60.

Spacks, Patricia Meyer. "Power and Meaning in *The Lord of the Rings*." Isaacs and Zimbardo, *Tolkien and the Critics*, 81-99.

Stanley, Charles. *The Blessings of Brokenness: Why God Allows Us to Go Through Tough Times*. Zondervan, 1997.

Steed, Robert. "The Harrowing of Hell Motif in Tolkien's Legendarium." *Mallorn* 58, 2017, 6-9.

Sterling, Grant. "The Consolation of Bilbo: Providence and Free Will in Middle-earth." Bassham and Bronson, 206-217.

Strauss, Ed. *A Hobbit Devotional*. Barbour, 2012.

Timco, Amy L. "Weavers, Witches, and Warriors: The Women of *The Lord of the Rings*." *Silver Leaves . . . from the White Tree of Hope*, issue 1, 2007, 39-45.

Timothy. "Riddles in the Dark." *Letters to C*, 28 Feb. 2017, letterstoc.com/2017/02/28/riddles-in-the-dark/. Accessed 25 May 2018.

---. "Roast Mutton." *Letters to C*, 7 Feb. 2017, letterstoc.com/2017/02/07/roast-mutton/. Accessed 25 May 2018.

Tolkien, J. R. R. "The Adventures of Tom Bombadil and other verses from The Red Book." *The Tolkien Reader*. Ballantine Books, 1966, 57-60.

---. *The Hobbit*. Illustrated by Jemina Caitlin. Houghton Mifflin Harcourt, 2013.

---. *The Letters of J. R. R. Tolkien*. Edited by Humphrey Carpenter, Houghton Mifflin, 2000.

---. *The Lord of the Rings*. 2nd ed., Houghton Mifflin, 1965-66.

---. *Morgoth's Ring: The History of Middle-earth, Vol. 10*. Edited by Christopher Tolkien, Houghton Mifflin, 1993.

---. "The Quest of Erebor." *Unfinished Tales of Númenor and Middle-earth*. Edited by Christopher Tolkien, Houghton Mifflin, 1980, 331-336.

---. *The Return of the Shadow: The History of* The Lord of the Rings, *Part 1*. Edited by Christopher Tolkien, Houghton Mifflin, 1988.

---. *Sauron Defeated: The History of* The Lord of the Rings, *Part 4*. Edited by Christopher Tolkien, Houghton Mifflin, 1992.

---. *The Silmarillion*. Edited by Christopher Tolkien, illustrated by Ted Nasmith, Houghton Mifflin, 2004.

---. *The Treason of Isengard: The History of* The Lord of the Rings, *Part 2*. Edited by Christopher Tolkien, Houghton Mifflin, 1989.

Topham, Nicole. "The Time That is Given to Us: Hope, Sacrifice, and Courage in *The Lord of the Rings*." Wells, I:327-331.

Wagner, Constance G. J. "Sacramentum Midgard: Frodo as Sacrament to Middle-earth." *Silver Leaves . . . from the White Tree of Hope*, issue 4, 2012, 83-87.

---. "The War Within: Frodo as Sacrificial Hero." Wells, I:338-342.

Ware, Jim. *Finding God in* The Hobbit. SaltRiver, 2006.

Wells, Sarah, editor. *The Ring Goes Ever On Proceedings of the Tolkien 2005 Conference: 50 Years of* The Lord of the Rings, 11-15 August 2005, Aston University, Birmingham, England, The Tolkien Society, 2008.

Wilkerson, Ginna. "So Far From the Shire: Psychological Distance and Isolation in *The Lord of the Rings*." *Mythlore*, vol. 27, no. 1/2, issue 103/104, 2008, 83-91.

Winter, Stephen C. "A Day of Praisegiving upon The Field of Cormallen." *Wisdom from The Lord of the Rings*, 20 Nov. 2017, stephencwinter.com/2017/11/20/a-day-of-praisegiving-upon-the-field-of-cormallen/. Accessed 10 Jun 2018.

---. "Frodo Finishes the Red Book and Gives it to Sam." *Wisdom from The Lord of the Rings,* 08 Aug. 2018, stephencwinter.com/2018/08/13/frodo-finishes-the-red-book-and-gives-it-to-sam/. Accessed 09 Sep. 2018.

---. "Frodo Gets Ready for The Feast at the Field of Cormallen," *Wisdom from The Lord of the Rings,* 27 Nov. 2017, stephencwinter.com/2017/11/27/7224/. Accessed 14 Jun 2018.

---. "Frodo and Sam Rest for a While in The Woods of Ithilien." *Wisdom from The Lord of the Rings,* 04 Dec. 2017, stephencwinter.com/2017/12/04/frodo-and-sam-rest-for-a-while-in-the-woods-of-ithilien/. Accessed 14 Jun 2018.

---. "Gollum Takes the Ring to the Fire." *Wisdom from The Lord of the Rings,* 16 Oct. 2017, stephencwinter.com/2017/10/16/gollum-takes-the-ring-to-the-fire/. Accessed 09 Jun 2018.

---. "Let Him Come and Open His Grief." *Wisdom from The Lord of the Rings,* 28 Apr. 2015, stephencwinter.com/2015/04/28/let-him-come-and-open-his-grief/. Accessed 03 June 2018.

---. "Sam asks 'Don't the Great Tales Never End?'" *Wisdom from The Lord of the Rings,* 01 Dec. 2015, stephencwinter.com/2015/12/01/sam-asks-dont-the-great-tales-never-end/. Accessed 30 May 2018.

---. "Saruman's Long Years of Death are Finally Revealed in His Corpse." *Wisdom from The Lord of the Rings,* 16 Jul 2018, stephencwinter.com/2018/07/16/sarumans-long-years-of-death-are-finally-revealed-in-his-corpse/. Accessed 10 Aug. 2018.

---. "Sauron and Frodo and Sam Show Us Two Different Relationships to Darkness." *Wisdom from The Lord of the Rings,* 11 Sep. 2017, stephencwinter.com/2017/09/11/sauron-and-frodo-and-sam-show-us-two-different-relationships-to-darkness/. Accessed 09 Jun 2018.

---. "Shagrat and Gorbag Carry Frodo to Mordor." *Wisdom from The Lord of the Rings*, 16 Feb. 2016, stephencwinter.com/2016/02/16/shagrat-and-gorbag-carry-frodo-to-mordor/. Accessed 17 Jun 2018.

---. "Sustained by a Longing for Beauty." *Wisdom from The Lord of the Rings*,3 Mar. 2015, stephencwinter.com/2015/03/03/sustained-by-a-longing-for-beauty/. Accessed 18 Sept. 2018.

Wood, Ralph C. "Conflict and Convergence on Fundamental Matters in C.S. Lewis and J.R.R. Tolkien." *The Free Library*, 22 June 2003, www.thefreelibrary.com/Conflict+and+convergence+on+fundamental+matters+in+C.S.+Lewis+and+...-a0109581099. Accessed 03 Jun 2018.

---. "Frodo's Faith." *Religion Online*, www.religion-online.org/article/frodos-faith/. Accessed 14 Jun 2018.

---. *The Gospel According to Tolkien: Visions of the Kingdom in Middle-earth.* Knox, 2003.

Wytenbroek, J. R. "Rites of Passage in *The Hobbit*." *Mythlore*, vol. 13, no. 4, issue 50, 1987, 5-8, 40.

Sneak Preview

A book of poems centered about a heroic quest and its aftermath

I step through
ringed door,

farewell the last farm,
homely light now behind us.

I breathe in the fresh air,
grasses tickle our feet,
a soft breeze brushes by.

The land lies

peaceful,
quiet,
unstained.

It knows not
its doom
passes nigh,

ready to
still its heart.

I must keep it this way.

This ring,
amidst many,
must not remain.

The night must swallow it,

or it will swallow the day.

CPSIA information can be obtained
at www.ICGtesting.com
Printed in the USA
FFHW022039281118
49681896-54073FF